BLESSED BEYOND THE CURSE

Donnie Clark

Copyright 2014 Donnie Clark

A religion that is small enough for our understanding is not great enough for our need.

Lord Arthur James Balfour

Index:

Chapter 1: I am tired, and you should be too
Recognizing that you were meant for more

Chapter 2: Am I cursed?
Understanding sin, blessing and the curse

Chapter 3: The Curse attached to unforgiveness
Learning the dangers of harboring bitterness

Chapter 4: The curse attached to unfruitfulness
You have one job: to bear fruit

Chapter 5: The blessing of appropriated honor
Inherit the blessing by honoring those above you

Chapter 6: The curse of robbing God
A Biblical explanation of the necessity of tithe and offerings

Chapter 7: The Blessing of True Integrity
Who you are when no one is looking really does matter

Chapter 8: The Jabez Blessing
More on you than it is on Him

Chapter 9: The Blessing of Enduring Faith
Pain is temporary. Quitting lasts forever

Chapter 1

I am tired. And you should be too

I am tired. Tired of living beneath my calling; tired of living beneath my standards; tired of living with compromise. I'm just tired. Can you relate? Maybe you have said things like, "this is not how my life was supposed to be", or "I never imagined myself doing this"? Many, probably most of us, are looking over the course of our lives, rather short, or long, and pondering the things we could have done differently, people we could have dated, jobs we could have taken, cars we should have bought, colors we should have painted the kitchen, and the list goes on and on. I am like that. My parents were like that. You are probably like that also. I spent my teenage years living in a backwoods South Alabama town right in the heart of the Bible belt where *everyone* went to church so that *everyone* could make it Heaven, as long as church was out by noon so *everyone* could make it to lunch on time.

I was saved by Jesus Christ and His precious blood at age thirteen, and baptized gloriously in His Holy Spirit four days later.

And I don't mean some little fall down on the floor and cry "baptism" (We didn't know we were supposed to fall until the mid-nineties). When I went to the altar at the young age of thirteen, I had no idea what I was asking for. And then, three or four older women, with long dresses, and long hair grabbed me, along with a couple older men in slacks and ties, and then commenced praying for me with a passion and a fervency that I can remember like it was yesterday. I had no instruction, I had no expectation, and I knew nothing. I just stood there and let them have their way with me, and boy they did! They prayed, and shouted, and danced, and did that little "whoo" that Pentecostals sometimes do. You know, that noise that they make when they get all "Holy Ghosted". They prayed over me for what felt like hours (it was literally about forty-five minutes), but somewhere in there, I felt something grab my spirit. That's really the best way I can describe it. It just reached into my chest and grabbed me, and it was heavy, and glorious. And I was changed.

    I began studying my King James Bible vigorously, and the words were coming alive to me. My grandfather, the preacher, gave me a plastic binder full of cassette tapes (google them kids, we lived by these things). These cassette tapes were the King James Bible on tape, being read in a monotone voice, as to not excite some fleshly reaction. I consumed it. I would play the tapes while reading along in my Bible. I would rewind them and listen again if I didn't understand it, or if those weird words didn't sound right to me. I would even hit play on my tape player each night before going to sleep and allow that monotone voice to speak the Living Word of God over me each night as I dreamed of whatever God had for me. I felt clean. I felt forgiven. I felt necessary.

That changed over the course of about two to three years. What happened to me? High School happened. I let go of all of that passion and traded it for the idolatry of my surroundings. I did what many of us do at that age, and that was try to define myself by all of the accoutrements that my environment afforded me. I bought the clothes that were in style, talked like the generation of cool kids, played the football jock, played the smooth *ladies' man*. But none of that defined me. All that did was plant seeds of confusion in the soil of my soul that had been so awakened to the power of Holy Spirit just a few years before. I carried those seeds, like a baby growing in the womb of their mother. I carried them, and they, like nature would have it, began to grow. I won't bore you with the details of my wanderings from the Lord, as they as typical and generic as anyone else's. But they did leave a mark on me. I never felt good enough, in all my trying to fit in. I always felt like someone was better at sports, better looking, had more money, and the list goes on. The insecurity inside of me was beyond familiar, it was now my identity. Every day I would awaken at five AM to lift weights because I wanted to look "buff". I would spend my entire paycheck on clothes to "keep up with the Jones". I drank alcohol if they were drinking, but I made sure I drank more. I smoked pot if they were smoking, but I made sure I was the highest. I slept with the whores because I wanted to be able to say that I had done that also. But I was miserably insecure. Miserably wishing someone would give me permission to not care about others' opinions. The entire time I'm dealing with the dull white noise of Holy Spirit constantly reminding me that I was meant for nothing that I was doing. But I learned to live with it like a rash that wouldn't go away, or a paralysis of a limb. It had just become something that was simply *there*.

Matthew 13:24-30

Jesus told them another parable: "The kingdom of heaven is like a man who sowed *good seed* in his field. But while everyone was *sleeping*, his enemy came and sowed weeds among the wheat, and went away. When the wheat sprouted and formed heads, then the weeds also appeared. "The owner's servants came to him and said, **'Sir, didn't you sow good seed in your field? Where then did the weeds come from?'** "'An enemy did this,' he replied. "The servants asked him, 'Do you want us to go and pull them up?' "'No,' he answered, 'because while you are pulling the weeds, you may uproot the wheat with them. **Let both grow together** until the harvest.

I fought against the wooing of Holy Spirit for a short time after graduating High School. I bounced from job to job, miserable with myself, and my life choices, never finding satisfaction in any occupation. Never finding contentment in any image I could create for myself. And then, after a couple years of marriage, and three or four jobs, I realized that the running had to end, and I had to embrace my calling. There were many more details to the process, but that's an entirely other book. The purpose of this synopsis is to show you a brief glimpse into how I got to the conclusions that I will make throughout the remainder of this book. Because when I said yes to the calling of God on my life, I had some issues. All those *seeds* that I planted in the soil of my soul for so many years had developed a firm root system and although I understood freedom, I also understood farming, and I understood while the Blood of Jesus had saved me, I still had to deal with the fruit of my choices.

What happened to me, and I supposed it happens to many of us, is that we get zealous for the Lord once we say yes to His will, and then we start to look for fruit and only see weeds that we allowed the enemy to plant at a moment of "sleeping". When these weeds are present in our lives, it creates a mindset of horizontal focus, rather than vertical response. Meaning that we tend to focus on everything around us, rather than simply responding to the Heavenlies as if you were sent from them. Many of us have developed an earthly mindset that has been carved there from constant exposure to a ground warfare. You war a spiritual battle from the ground, therefore your reality is based on what you see and experience. So, for some of you, although the word says you can do *all things* through Christ who strengthens you, you feel as though you can do *a few things* through my own strength. Although the word tells you that you are the head, not the tail, but you "feel like" a whipped tail. You know the scriptures, and you know that sickness cannot reign in you, but you are always sick. You know that cancer and disease has to bow to the name of Jesus, but apparently, they've never heard of you. And when your position on spiritual things is *trapped* in your mindset of what you see, you are not only NOT living according to the promise of the Word, but you are not acting in any kind of Godlike faith whatsoever. And when that mindset has taken root in you, you will always allow your situation to determine your attitude.

It's the journey that creates the value, not the title.

Calling myself a pastor didn't cause me to live up to being a pastor. Calling myself a husband didn't make me a husband. Father, friend, worshipper, teacher; none of those gave me a security to be any of them. Titles are false securities that only further the frustration of this walk because they force you to now live up to the standard that many before you, who wore that title much better than you, lived. But seeing that certificate with the *REV.* in front of my name only caused anxiety in me. It made me think that the title was too cheaply given. I achieved it with little effort. I felt I hadn't earned the right to be a real pastor. I didn't value it because it was now attached to me, and I was nothing, no one.

Then I walked a while in those shoes. And I learned that it's not the title that makes you valuable, it's the journey that makes the title worth it. Going through hell to develop that word in me caused me to value it. It's the same with the word of God over our lives. I am an overcomer, and **NOT** because the word says so. The word saying so simply gave me the faith that became the infrastructure to step out into what I didn't see and walk through tests and trials to get to the place where I overcame, and now, because I walked through things, I truly belief that I can overcome. I place value in that ability. But it was because I had to walk it, and it's the journey that makes it valuable. If your mindset is earthly focused, your conclusion is that there is no hope. But the word says, that "even when we were dead in trespasses, (we were) made us alive together with Christ (by grace you have been saved), and raised *us* up together, and made *us* sit together in the heavenly *places* in Christ Jesus." (*Ephesians 2:5-6 NKJV*). That's not future, that's now. Teaching us that you can be positioned correctly, in order to see correctly, and then you can respond correctly. Because although you see this world as something horrible and you're barely making it through, the Bible says in Isaiah 6:1-3

"In the year that King Uzziah died, I saw the Lord sitting on a throne, high and lifted up, and the train of His *robe* filled the temple. Above it stood seraphim; each one had six wings: with two he covered his face, with two he covered his feet, and with two he flew. And one cried to another and said:

"Holy, holy, holy *is* the LORD of hosts; **The whole earth *is* full of His glory!"**

Seraphim, which are positioned in *His presence,* see the earth full of HIS GLORY. That right there is just amazing. Because you, positioned where you are may see your life as all hell breaking loose, but the ones who are in HIS presence are saying the "Whole earth" is FULL of His glory, so one of us is wrong.

The goal of this book is to expose you to biblical curses, and teach you the purpose of blessing, and how it has the power to remove that curse from your life, and then it's up to you. The weed is going to grow with the wheat, but then you have a choice.

"At that time I will tell the harvesters: First collect the weeds and **tie them in bundles to be burned**; then gather the wheat and bring it into my barn.'" (Matthew 13:30)

"Bless his Little Heart"

James 3:9-12 says,
"With the tongue we praise our Lord and Father, and with it we curse human

beings, who have been made in God's likeness. Out of the same mouth come praise and cursing. My brothers and sisters, this should not be. Can both fresh water and salt water flow from the same spring? My brothers and sisters, can a fig tree bear olives, or a grapevine bear figs? Neither can a salt spring produce fresh water."

When we think of blessing, we think immediately of money, but money is a small part of blessing. To make money the totality of the word blessing is anti the word of God. To understand what "blessing" is, is to understand that blessing is a work of redemption.

Galatians 3:13-14
"Christ has **redeemed** us from the **curse** of the law, having become a curse for us (for it is written, "Cursed *is* everyone who hangs on a tree"), that the blessing of Abraham might come upon the Gentiles in Christ Jesus, that we might receive the promise of the Spirit through faith."

The curse takes away what we were deemed for. The blessing RE-DEEMS us to be positioned to be what we were originally deemed to become. If you were deemed to be the manager of a business, and then through some misconduct or inappropriate behavior you were dismissed from that position is a picture of what sin does to us. It removes us from our ordained position. However, redemption happens when you are exonerated of all wrong doing, reinstated to your previous position, and treated as if it had never happened. That is the beauty of redemption. It puts us right back where we belong, regardless of the mistake we made. As with anything I teach, I implore you to not only hear with your ears, and comprehend with you mind, but to actually take steps to walk this thing into application. Because no one wants to live under a curse. We all want to live under the full God-ordained blessing that He has prepared for us. So, for the next few moments, I want to bring definition and understanding to these concepts, and then we'll run with it after we build a little foundation.

"No one would allow garbage at his table, but many allow it served into their minds."
Fulton John Sheen

The scripture reference I mentioned earlier in James (3:9-12) is foundational in this book, and in understanding how to be BLESSED beyond the curse. It is foundational because James is trying to show us the principle that all blessing is done with a release of the words of your mouth. And he is also showing us that all cursing is done with the release of the words of your mouth. That out of the abundance of the heart, the mouth speaks (Proverbs 4:23). Think about that for a moment. That what is coming out of your mouth is literally coming from the abundance, or the overflowing of the affections of your heart. Not a small portion of your affections, but the overflow. So when anger is released, it's not something that slips out of you, it has been filling you higher and higher until finally, you are overflowing with anger. It's an overflowing, not a slip up. If you are always talking negatively about every situation, it is more than just a "bad day", it is the flowing over of what is inside of your heart. Out of the overflowing of your true affection, you produce your words.

For I know that my Redeemer lives, and that at the last he will stand upon the earth. Job 19:25

Chapter 2:

Am I cursed?

"Maybe the atheist cannot find God for the same reason a thief cannot find a policeman."

unknown

Most people don't bother worrying about this because they would actually then be required to do something about it! But hopefully by the time you make it to Chapter two, you've actually got a little spark inside of you to get this monkey off your back! So let's just jump right into this and I want to show you some key thought about the curse.

And yes, you can steal it and preach it, teach it, whatever, and even say you came up with it, I do not care. *(Just don't publish it, it's copyrighted)*

1. The curse is a response to, or the fruit of sin

Psalm 119:11 - I treasure your word in my heart, so that I may not sin against you.

Genesis 3:14
So the LORD God said to the serpent: "Because you have done this, you *are* cursed more than all cattle, and more than every beast of the field; on your belly you shall go, and you shall eat dust all the days of your life.

Now let's look down at verses 17-19:
Then to Adam He said, "Because you have heeded the voice of your wife, and have eaten from the tree of which I commanded you, saying, 'You shall not eat of it': "Cursed *is* the ground for your sake; in toil you shall eat *of* it all the days of your life. Both thorns and thistles it shall bring forth for you, and you shall eat the herb of the field. In the sweat of your face you shall eat bread till you return to the ground, for out of it you were taken; for dust you *are,* and to dust you shall return."

Sin is literally the doorway to the curse. God releases the curse through His mouth as a response to sin. The curse was released by the mouth of God. Such power in the spoken word! Look at this; in Genesis 4, when Cain murders Abel, verses 10-12 say, "And He said, "What have you done? The voice of your brother's blood cries out to Me from the ground. So now you *are* cursed from the earth, which has opened its mouth to receive your brother's blood from your hand. When you till the ground, it shall no longer yield its strength to you. A fugitive and a vagabond you shall be on the earth." Sin is the doorway to the curse. David was cursed with the death of his firstborn because of his sin. Solomon began to *number* horses and wives; Samson didn't take his vow serious; Hiel of Bethel rebuilt Jericho.

"The root of sin is indolence of heart."
Alan Ecclestone

What is sin?

1 John 3:4-6
    Whoever commits sin also commits *lawlessness,* and *sin is lawlessness.* And you know that He was manifested to take away our sins, and in Him there is no sin. Whoever abides in Him does not sin. Whoever sins has neither seen Him nor known Him.

"Sin is the dare of God's justice, the rape of his mercy, the jeer of his patience, the slight of his power, and the contempt of his love."
John Bunyan

I have a good friend, and brother in the Lord named Casey Doss. Casey is the Pastor of the Ramp School of Ministry, and Pastors at the Ramp Church in Hamilton, Alabama, under the leading of Karen Wheaton. Casey began to express how grossly we misjudge the concept of sin in this little excerpt from a conference we hosted that he was a speaker at:

"All of y'all need Jesus. You pray six hours a day? That's fantastic, you still need Jesus. You addicted to alcohol? That's okay, you need Jesus too. You went to seminary? Oh my goodness! You need Jesus too. You got more degrees behind your name than a thermometer! That's fantastic, but you still need Jesus too! You been ordained through the Assemblies of God! Wonderful, but you still need Jesus! You came to the Ramp School of Ministry! YOU NEED JESUS!!!"

None of us are exempt from the need of a Savior to take our sinful nature away and put the nature of true love inside of us.

Sin is not a list of things to do or don't do. It's simply lawlessness, or going against, *or without*, the law God gives you. And it is not exclusive to your preference.

It bothers me greatly when Christian leaders classify sin based on their own judgments of it. For example, most (I wish I could say all). But most American Evangelical pastors claim that homosexuality is a blatant sin, and would never perform a wedding for two homosexuals. However, how many of those same pastors have, and do perform weddings for two heterosexual people who are living in sexual sin? How many people "rent" the church, "rent" the pastor, "rent" the decorator for their wedding, to make it look like a Christian wedding, when it's not at all Christian? What that does, is justify how money driven we are, that if the price is right, we'll compromise our convictions for the almighty dollar. But homosexual sin is no different from heterosexual sin in the eyes of God. He does not have different compartments of hell for the homosexual that keeps them separated from the heterosexual. I decided many years ago that I would not marry anyone that was not actively producing Kingdom fruit in their lives. I just won't do it. I'm accountable to God for what I pronounce a blessing over in His name. And for the record, I am not for homosexual marriage. In fact we have had several homosexuals come to our church and some of them even get mad at me because I do not get upset about them being homosexual because "that's what preachers do". They want me to get mad so they can argue that sin is sin to God, but I argue it first and they are left with just that. Sin is sin. It's knowing the good you should do and not doing it (James 4:17). That's it. Nothing more, nothing less. So throw out the list. All the list did was make you aware of how bad you really are.

Romans 7:7-8 NIV

What shall we say, then? Is the law sinful? Certainly not! Nevertheless, I would not have known what sin was had it not been for the law. For ***I would not have known what coveting really was if the law had not said, "You shall not covet."*** But sin, seizing the opportunity afforded by the commandment, produced in me every kind of coveting. For apart from the law, sin was dead.

Sin, or Lawlessness, is the door that opens in front of you that causes you to walk in the curse. The lie from the very beginning has been that you get a preference in this Christianity walk. Let me break your American dream guised in the wolf skin of "the Church of America"; **you don't get it your way**.

The word *"preference"* means that you determine if, how, and when you respond to the word given to you. But EVERY word of God demands a response. So, when a minister stands in a pulpit and delivers a word from God, you respond, or you move into lawlessness, or sin. And I know this seems harsh, but God takes sin seriously, and He is a God of order.

What blessing are you missing because you are walking in preference, which is compromise, which is lawlessness, which is sin?

Deuteronomy 11:26 NKJV
"Behold, I set before you today a blessing and a curse: the blessing, if you obey the commandments of the L ord your God

which I command you today; and the curse, if you do not obey the commandments of the LORD your God, but turn aside from the way which I command you today, to go after other gods which you have not known."

"The result of continued disobedience is deeper bondage" – Damon Thompson

Walking in the curse is simply a response to your choice to engage in sin.

2. <u>The power of words will span generations</u>

Numbers 14:18
'The LORD is longsuffering and abundant in mercy, forgiving iniquity and transgression; but He by no means clears *the guilty,* visiting the iniquity of the fathers on the children to the third and fourth *generation.*'

If you understood the power in releasing curses and blessing, it would change everything about what you chose to release.

Proverbs 17:27-28

He who has knowledge spares his words, *and* a man of understanding is of a calm spirit. Even a fool is counted wise when he holds his peace; *when* he shuts his lips, *he is considered* perceptive.

The release of blessing and curses shape the course of people's lives. This is why the beloved James spends the first 6 verses of chapter 3 of his writing talking about how the tongue can change the course of all that it encounters. That bits in horses mouths are small, yet control the entire movement of the horse. So are the tongue and the words you speak. That ships are steered by a small rudder, and that entire forests are set ablaze by a small spark, as such is the power of the tongue.

Not only does James show us the proportion of size between the tongue and what it can affect, but he is also showing us the damage that the tongue can do in changing the literal course and purpose.

I had a prophetic word for our church a while back and I think it needs to be heard. In my spirit, I saw a large ship that had huge eyes in the front of it. It was sitting still in the middle of the ocean just staring out into the great expanse in front of it. When The Lord showed me this I heard him say that although you have vision (eyes) for your assignment, and although the means (ship, finances, favor) is there, you are not fulfilling it because your rudder has been destroyed because of your negative talk. You release a curse over every plan I have simply because you cannot "see it" being able to happen in your own eyes, therefore releasing the curse over your assigned purpose.

And what's even more detrimental is that the enemy knows the power of the word, especially when it comes to generational assignments. Genesis 9:18 tells us, "Now the sons of Noah who went out of the ark were Shem, Ham, and Japheth. And Ham *was* the father of Canaan." Notice that the detail of Ham's child's name was given in this portion of the scripture. Now, if you skip down to verse 22, you see the same association of Ham to his son, Canaan: "And Ham, the father of Canaan, saw the nakedness of his father, and told his two brothers outside."

But look at what happens next, in verse 24, it says that "Noah awoke from his wine, and knew what his younger son had done to him. Then he said: "**Cursed *be* Canaan**; a servant of servants he shall be to his brethren." Abraham released a curse over Ham for his sin, and completely neglected to even mention Ham, he went straight to his son, Canaan. Showing us the power of words, that it wasn't just the curse on HAM, but that it was a curse on the generations that followed Ham.

Understand the power that your words have for generations. Girls who have no self-worth are walking in this defeated mind battle because their grandmother walked in a curse. Men and boys are struggling daily with perversion and pornography addiction because their fathers had secret sin, and kept magazines under the bed, or watched X-rated movies on television while you were a child sleeping in the next room. Don't think that what you do stops with you, it doesn't.

If you're old enough to have children, you see how much they are like you. They talk like you, act like you, have the same tastes in things, admire the same entertainment. All because they are a release of *your word* in the earth.

Fathers, is your orgasm worth their future?

"A portion of guilt is standard issue for southern boys; our whole lives are convoluted, egregious apologies to our mothers because our fathers have made us such flawed husbands."
Pat Conroy, The Prince of Tides

3. <u>Those who are blessed gain the authority to release the blessing from them.</u>

Numbers 6:24-26
"The LORD *bless you* and keep you; the LORD make his face shine on you and be gracious to you; the LORD turn his face toward you and give you peace."

Genesis 12:2 says, "I will make you a great nation; I will *bless you* and make your name great; and ***you shall be a blessing***."

This is beautiful. God is telling Abraham, in essence, "The reason I am blessing you, is so that you will be positioned to release a blessing yourself." This is the beauty of the Word of God, and the power of His grace in our lives! That when He decides to release blessing on you, it removes the curse, and positions you to be a blessing.

Galatians 3:8-9

And the Scripture, foreseeing that God would justify the Gentiles by faith, preached the gospel to Abraham beforehand, *saying,* "In you all the nations shall be blessed." So then those who *are* of faith are blessed with believing Abraham.

Mind = Blown.

How do we know if you are walking in blessing? When you are positioned to release a curse over someone, and instead you release blessing over them. When the fruit of your life is that you are restoring when you could have cursed and condemned. It is our vocation as the people of God, to release blessing, because it releasing the redemptive work of God in the world. It is *you* removing the curse, because *you* are the seed of Abraham.

"God doesn't bless us just to make us happy; He blesses us to make us into a blessing."
Warren W. Wiersbe

1 Peter 3:8-12 *The Message*

"Be agreeable, be sympathetic, be loving, be compassionate, be humble. That goes for all of you, no exceptions. No retaliation. No sharp-tongued sarcasm. Instead, bless—that's your job, to bless. You'll be a blessing and also get a blessing."

The natural result of being blessed of God is to turn around and bless others. That is fruit, and fruit doesn't lie. If you're not blessing others, then you can surmise very quickly without much effort that you are not walking in blessing. God wants to bless you, but you have to understand the reason behind the blessing. In the world we live in, you're rich if you have money and all your bills are paid, and you can buy whatever you want, but in the Kingdom, you're only rich if you're able to take care of the community. Solomon was rich, David was rich. Jesus was rich, and He had to get His tax money from the mouth of fish, but He was rich, because the measuring stick of the Kingdom is how much you can bless others.

And you lose that authority to walk in blessing when you are positioned to release blessing and chose not to. How many times are we sitting at a red light and there is a homeless person standing there holding a sign that says, "Will work for food", or "homeless, please help"? We see this all the time and our conscious will not allow us to even look at them. And we keep our eyes forward as we drive past them looking for anything in the world to shift our focus towards because we don't want to deal with the reality that we can help them, we just don't want to. And that's the real reason, we just don't want to.

We even make excuses like, "Well, they're just going to use the money to buy alcohol". When, in reality, you're just going to use it to feed your flesh also, but since you "earned" it, you can use that excuse. Regardless of what they do with it, it's your job to be obedient to bless. We make ourselves judge when we withhold blessing because we don't think they measure up to the standard we have for releasing a blessing.

Now, I understand if you don't have it, but most of us do have something to give, and there are countless other examples that I could use, but I'm sure you're squirming right now, so I'll move on.

The only way we walk in blessing is to be a blessing to others. Period.

4. The curse can negate the blessing just like the blessing can negate the curse

You can have a word, or promise, or a blessing, and the doorway, or the window, or whatever metaphoric access point to it can be blocked by your own sin. Because of this principle: a curse has the ability to remove the blessing, and a blessing has the ability to remove the curse.

Genesis 12:1-3 says that "the LORD had said to Abram: "Get out of your country, from your family and from your father's house, to a land that I will show you. I will make you a great nation; I will bless you and make your name great; and you shall be a blessing. I will bless those who bless you, and I will curse him who curses you; and in you all the families of the earth shall be blessed."

Do you ever wonder why the Bible doesn't say much from Adam to Abraham? You should for the simple fact that from Adam to Abraham is a couple thousand years! That's a lot of time to cover and not have much detail.

The reason why we don't hear much is (I believe) because the whole earth is under the curse of Adam. No one has released the blessing of God; they've just continued to walk in the curse. That doesn't give you much to talk about. If it weren't for Noah (The drunken guy), our Bibles would not have the same starting point, if we would even be here. The earth had stood under the curse of Adam for a long time. The people have toiled and tried to produce something and have not been able to do anything. So, when there's nothing good to say, nothing is said. So, really, what we have is a bunch of chapters that give us validation of the genealogical chart that gets us from Adam to Abraham. Or the way I like to see it is that it's a map to get us from curse to blessing.

"Our society strives to avoid any possibility of offending anyone - except God."
Billy Graham

How does the curse end? The curse ends when God, who was the offended party, choses to not be offended by the sin of Adam, and choses to bless instead of curse. God was the offended one. He had every right to continue to curse the people because of their sin. But he made a choice to forgive and to release a blessing from his mouth when he had every right to release a curse. You need to understand that just because you have the right, and you were offended, and they done you wrong and life is not fair, or just because you can justify it, you have a choice to release blessing or cursing over people.

God was the offended one, and he had every right to continue cursing humanity. I keep saying this because I want you to get it. But one word of blessing from the offended One released the curse for humanity. Before Abraham, the world was living under a curse, but now, since the Father released a blessing, there is hope, there is movement, there is a light of understanding that we don't have to be like this forever.

There are people that cannot walk in blessing because you continue to curse them. It is through blessing, that we can redeem those who are cursed. And we have a responsibility to bless people because the REDEMPTIVE work of God is carried out by his people.

Matthew 5:44 says, "But I say to you, love your enemies, bless those who curse you, do good to those who hate you, and pray for those who spitefully use you and persecute you." A lot of times we are not sure what to do with that scripture. We restrain our mouths from blessing because we feel like if we bless a situation that is outside the will of God that we are putting our stamp of approval on it. And when people curse us, we are not sure really what it means to bless them back, because we don't want them to be financially abundant in their cursing of us.

Also, when people mistreat us, or they are living in compromise, we don't want to bless them because you don't want to come into agreement with a situation that is outside of the will of God. While I do understand those reasonings (and I have used all of them in my own pleading case to avoid blessing enemies), the reason we have a responsibility to bless those who curse us is because if we restrain our lips from blessing, we are restraining the redemptive work of God in that situation. Many times we want to wait until the situation lines up with the will of God before we bless them. But if you would start blessing them, the situation will line up with the will of God, because it's the blessing that breaks off the curse.

It is the blessing that releases the power of God to redeem the situation. It is the blessing, not your gossip that changes the situation. It is our blessing, not our cursing that draws people to the Lord. When you restrain your lips from blessing, or worse, if you curse back, what you are doing is, you're allowing the sin of Adam, and the effects of the curse to endure.

Romans 12:2
    Do not be conformed to this world, but be transformed by the renewing of your minds, so that you may discern what is the will of God.

It's time! Time to awaken yourself to action. Time to stop giving into "life" and what it has thrown at you, and time to decide that you will no longer house the curse, but you will release the blessing of God over your family, your community, your church, and yourself!

Chapter 3:

The Curse attached to my unforgiveness

"Worst of all my foes, I fear the enemy within."
John Wesley

James 3:9-12

"With the tongue we praise our Lord and Father, and with it we curse human beings, who have been made in God's likeness. Out of the same mouth come praise and cursing. My brothers and sisters, this should not be. Can both fresh water and salt water flow from the same spring? My brothers and sisters, can a fig tree bear olives, or a grapevine bear figs? Neither can a salt spring produce fresh water."

A "blessing" is a work of redemption. It redeems. It takes what we were deemed for, that we messed up, and it places it right back on us as if it were never removed. Galatians 3:13-14 tells us that "Christ has redeemed us from the curse of the law, having become a curse for us (for it is written, "Cursed *is* everyone who hangs on a tree"), that the blessing of Abraham might come upon the

Gentiles in Christ Jesus, that we might receive the promise of the Spirit through faith." The curse takes away what we were deemed for. The blessing RE-DEEMS us to be positioned to be what we were originally deemed to become.

The word "Blessing" in Hebrew means, **"The beneficial ingredient of power to produce wellbeing in every aspect of life."** It is a literal force in your life that is released. Proverbs 10:22 says, "The blessing of the LORD makes *one* rich, and He adds no sorrow with it." When God blesses you, He is releasing a "Beneficial ingredient" into us. His blessing is beneficial! That should make you want to run around a room or something.

Matthew 18:21-35:
    Then came Peter to him, and said, Lord, how oft shall my brother sin against me, and I forgive him? Till seven times? Jesus saith unto him, I say not unto thee, Until seven times: but, Until seventy times seven. Therefore is the kingdom of heaven likened unto a certain king, which would take account of his servants. And when he had begun to reckon, one was brought unto him, which owed him ten thousand talents. But forasmuch as he had

not to pay, his lord commanded him to be sold, and his wife, and children, and all that he had, and payment to be made. The servant therefore fell down, and worshipped him, saying, Lord, have patience with me, and I will pay thee all. Then the lord of that servant was moved with compassion, and loosed him, and forgave him the debt. But the same servant went out, and found one of his fellowservants, which owed him an hundred pence: and he laid hands on him, and took him by the throat, saying, Pay me that thou owest. And his fellowservant fell down at his feet, and besought him, saying, Have patience with me, and I will pay thee all.

And he would not: but went and cast him into prison, till he should pay the debt. So when his fellowservants saw what was done, they were very sorry, and came and told unto their lord all that was done. Then his lord, after that he had called him, said unto him, O thou wicked servant, I forgave thee all that debt, because thou desiredst me:

Shouldest not thou also have had compassion on thy fellowservant, even as I had pity on thee? And his lord was wroth, and delivered him to the tormentors, till he should pay all that was due unto him. So likewise shall my heavenly Father do also unto you, if ye from your hearts forgive not everyone his brother their trespasses.

First of all, understand that Peter gets a bad rap sometimes for his impulsiveness and aggressive response to Jesus. But Peter was actually being Biblically accurate with this statement because Proverbs 6:30-31 tells us "*People* do not despise a thief if he steals to satisfy himself when he is starving. Yet *when* he is found, he must restore sevenfold".

Peter is recognizing the equal and just requirement for someone who sins against you, that they repay 7 fold. But God is not a God of equal or enough, but a God of more than enough. His name is *El Shaddai* - God Almighty, source of all blessing, the God of more than enough. He even justifies His name with His statement in Luke 6:38 where He tells us to "Give, and it will be given to you: **good measure, pressed down, shaken together, and running over** will be put into your bosom. For with the same measure that you use, it will be measured back to you."

Matthew 13:8 says "But other fell into good ground, and brought forth fruit, some an hundredfold, some sixtyfold, some thirtyfold". When the widow had just enough oil, Elisha blessed her, and not only did she have "enough", but the prophet told her not just to pay her debts, but to live off of the rest!! That's the kind of God we serve. There's something amazing about the nature of God that he always wants to do "more than necessary", while we strive to do a little less than "necessary" and call it good enough. Ephesians 3:20 says, "Now to Him who is able to do exceedingly abundantly above all that we ask or think, according to the power that works in us"!

He wants to BE the God of more than enough, but His ability to do that is limited by the amount of "Power that works in us". For example, I have a lawn mower that is small, and cheap, and sometimes runs, and sometimes decides not to for no other reason than it just does not want to crank. It has a little power, and it takes me several hours to mow my yard. I have a friend who has a lawn business, and he has a super charged, zero turn yard destroyer, that goes as fast as some small foreign cars. His ability to produce more is fueled by his investing in the power behind it.

Excess.

Peter is actually heading down the right path, he's using scripture, but Jesus says, no, that's appropriate according to the law, but I came to fulfill the law. If you want to do it right, let's get excessive in this. He illustrates how to remove the curse that is attached with our unforgiveness through the power of blessing through this parable.

The man in the story:
The man in this story is guilty of an offense. He deserved judgment and he could not pay the debt that he legitimately owed due to his own actions. He could beg, but begging didn't settle the debt, although we think it does! How many of us cry out to God when the weeds start showing and the debtors start calling? Begging didn't move the Judge. He could cry, but crying wouldn't settle the debt. This is a giant telescope into our souls of how we react when we are offended by someone. They can apologize, but we still feel wronged. They can ask for forgiveness and we will even lie to them and say it's no big deal.

You will turn around and start re-hashing the conversation in your head about what you really feel and how you wished you had told them what you think, and how you will "love them but I don't have to like them." Start playing scenarios where they ask you for a favor, and you're like, "I'm sorry I can't, you suck." And then you hang up and say, "That's what you get for what you did to me." Sound familiar? This is you trying to produce fruit in cursed ground. Adam couldn't do it. Cain couldn't do it. Noah couldn't do it. And you cannot do it. And you "warning" other people about what someone did to you because you "just don't want to see it happen to them" is not bringing honor to God.

Romans 12:17-21

Repay no one evil for evil. Have regard for good things in the sight of all men. If it is possible, as much as depends on you, live peaceably with all men. Beloved, do not avenge yourselves, but *rather* give place to wrath; for it is written, "Vengeance *is* Mine, I will repay," says the Lord. Therefore "If your enemy is hungry, feed him; If he is thirsty, give him a drink; For in so doing you will heap coals of fire on his head." Do not be overcome by evil, but overcome evil with good.

Ephesians 4:30-32

And do not grieve the Holy Spirit of God, by whom you were sealed for the day of redemption. Let all bitterness, wrath, anger, clamor, and evil speaking be put away from you, with all malice. And be kind to one another, tenderhearted, forgiving one another, even as God in Christ forgave you.

It literally grieves the Holy Spirit when you hold onto your offense. Why? Simply put, because of the weight and scale of your forgiveness. Let's look again at Matthew 18, beginning in verse 26:

The servant therefore fell down, and worshipped him, saying, Lord, have patience with me, and I will pay thee all. Then the lord of that servant was moved with compassion, and loosed him, and forgave him the debt. But the same servant went out, and found one of his fellowservants, which owed him an hundred pence: and he laid hands on him, and took him by the throat, saying, Pay me that thou owest. And his fellowservant fell down at his feet, and besought him, saying, Have patience with me, and I will pay thee all. And he would not: *but went and cast him into prison, till he should pay the debt.*

But if the man is in prison, there's no way he can work to pay off the debt. And this is EXACTLY what it looks like when you attempt to hold onto unforgiveness for someone who may have offended you. Because unforgiveness locks people behind the prison door of your opinion of them. And as long as they stay locked away there, there is no way they can work to pay off that debt.

People that offended you five years ago are still imprisoned by your opinion of them based solely on that offence. And they may have grown, and learned from that time, and become mature, and moved on, and may be doing well with their life, and the whole time they are exactly who you thought them to be at the time of the offence, because offence locks them in the dungeon of your mind, and as long as they are trapped there, they can never get free in order to provide a way to make penance with you.

In other words, regardless of what they do in their own life to better themselves, they will always be the person that hurt you. They can pastor the greatest church in your town, and anytime someone mentions them, you immediately spit venom talking about what he did to you eight years ago, and "he don't know how to council people", or "he didn't come to the hospital when I had surgery", or whatever stupid offence that you had so many years ago has locked him into that view that you have created, and he may be the one you're actually called to support and serve, in order to walk in your blessing! Listen to me today, friend, they will NEVER change in your book because you have them locked away.

They could even try to make contact with you, and you would brush them off and even try to diminish their efforts by attaching a "wrong motive" to their actions. Saying crazy things like, "They only trying to talk to me because they want my money". Or, "I know he don't mean what he's saying, he ain't changed". How arrogantly ridiculous is it of us to imprison someone who is making progress in their life by the offence that they may, or may not be aware of committing in times past? The reality is that it's not them in prison; it's you, and their just visiting an old friend in jail who wants to blame everyone else as to why you are in the misery you call life. That, my friend is walking in the curse of unforgiveness.

Back to the scripture, we see in verses 34 & 35, the curse:

"And his lord was wroth, and delivered him to the tormentors, till he should pay all that was due unto him. So likewise shall my heavenly Father do also unto you, if ye from your hearts forgive not everyone his brother their trespasses."

You need to get a revelation of how Kingdom things work. This scripture teaches us that "Tormenting spirits" (*The tormentors*) are granted access to YOU, by permission of God, because of your unforgiveness! Now, all us good, Bible belt, Sunday morning "go to meeting" clothes wearing, fried chicken eating, self-indulged, good intentioned "Christians" would all agree that a Christian cannot be possessed by a demon. That light and darkness cannot co-exist. And that's how "black and white" everything is in our Southern, American, middle class, white, yuppie, home schooled, granola bar eating, bottled water drinking society. That if it's demonic, it's a demon in you, and if it's a demon in you, you must have hidden sin, and we're going to condemn you and guilt you into confessing something because there's no way you can just be "tormented".

There is no mention of demonic possession, but something I think we tend to overlook because we think God is more like Mr. Rogers wanting to be our neighbor.

His unforgiveness caused God to judge him according to his heart, and because that was there, it unlocked doors to tormenting spirits whose only job is to mess with your mind day and night. Have you ever been there? Just constant mental attacks. Just constant feelings of bitterness. Constant worry and anxiety, depression, and just a sour anger gnawing at you constantly because you cannot forgive them for what they did, even though they are fine with life… You are living in constant torment.

Notice that nothing you are producing in this state of being is considered to be fruit of the spirit, yet some of you deal with these on a consistent basis. Let's take a REAL LOOK at who you really are, *Christian*. If you can tell a tree by the fruit that it bears (Matthew 7:16-17), then are you really the one who is in the right? Are you? Or could it be that you are simply one step away from releasing all of those negative tormenting things in your life, simply by forgiving?

And because you've been taught that a Christian cannot be demonized, and they cannot, you assume it's just part of life's struggle. That *"Paul had his thorn in his flesh, and God must think I'm capable of handling this, for His glory, of course."* (Sarcasm added, offence intended). How arrogant to even begin to classify ourselves within the same category as Paul, He was stoned to death in one of his first missionary journeys, and raised up again to preach in the same city that stoned him.

You're holding onto bitterness because some visitor took your spot in the puke green pew one Sunday and the pastor didn't ask them to move because, after all, "you are a pillar of that church." (I use the example of Pastors, and church for two reasons, first of all, because I am a pastor, and I can talk about myself, and secondly, that seems to be the greatest area of offence. The same thing could happen in a work place, and we move on like nothing happened. Don't get me started chasing that rabbit).

You're not demonized. The reality is that you may be saved, going to Heaven, and making some attempt at Christianity. But you have all this fruit that is just plain ugly. Let's call it what it is. And the root is that you, *who have been forgiven from the curse*, still harbor the unforgiveness of the offense that you received.

Forgiveness involves three elements

There are three elements to walking out forgiveness. First there must be an *injury*. Secondly, there must develop a *debt* resulting from that injury. And thirdly, there must produce a *cancellation of that debt* by the offended party.

Most of the time, when you are under the curse of unforgiveness, you don't even realize that is the root of your problem. All you know is that if I say their name, something inside of you shifts, and moves, and you get uneasy. And that point right there was like the grand slam in the ninth inning! It just made sense didn't it? Something moves in you when you say their name or think of them. That's the bitter root of unforgiveness.

Mark 11:25-26 NKJV
"And whenever you stand praying, if you have anything against anyone, forgive him, that your Father in heaven may also

forgive you your trespasses. But if you do not forgive, neither will your Father in heaven forgive your trespasses."

Matthew 5:23-24 NKJV
 Therefore if you bring your gift to the altar, and there remember that your brother has something against you, leave your gift there before the altar, and go your way. First be reconciled to your brother, and then come and offer your gift.

Proverbs 20:22 NKJV
 Do not say, "I will recompense evil"; wait for the LORD, and He will save you.

Luke 7:47 NKJV
 Therefore I say to you, her sins, which *are* many, are forgiven, for she loved much. But to whom little is forgiven, *the same* loves little."

Ephesians 1:7 NKJV
 In Him we have redemption through His blood, the forgiveness of sins, according to the riches of His grace.

 It truly is a blessing to be able to look at someone and not allow their actions to offend you. That we would be like Jesus, who rebuked Peter for attacking the guards by saying, "Put up thy sword into the sheath: the cup which my Father hath given me, shall I not drink it?" That Jesus was so dead to offence that even a kiss from a betrayer who once was a friend was viewed by Christ as "A cup from my Father."

That's freedom. That's walking in the blessing. That's Christianity. That's revolutionary. That's empowerment, and that's who we are to be. It's far more beautiful to forgive, and restore, than to walk in a curse, because you harbor bitterness.

To quote my beautiful 2 year old granddaughter, Emma Grace. "let it doe, let it doe" (Her favorite movie this month is "Frozen".

Break the curse.

Forgive.

Forget.

> "I can forgive, but I cannot forgive" is only another way of saying, "I cannot forgive."
> Henry Ward Beecher

Psalm 103:12

As far as the east is from the west, so far hath he removed our transgressions from us.

Micah 7:19

He will turn again, he will have compassion upon us; he will subdue our iniquities; and thou wilt cast all their sins into the depths of the sea.

That doesn't mean be ignorant. If someone molests your child (sorry to paint such a graphic picture), but if that were to happen, you don't ignorantly hire them as a babysitter because "We gotta forgive and forget". No, you use wisdom, but forgiveness is strictly about forgetting what their action did to you. It's about literally letting go of that because you were a different person then, and hopefully so were they.

Let it go.

Forgive.

Forget.

Walk in blessing.

And be kind to one another, tenderhearted,
forgiving one another, as God in Christ Jesus
has forgiven you.
Ephesians 4:32

Chapter 4:

The Curse attached to my unfruitfulness

Then God blessed them, and God said to them, "Be fruitful and multiply; fill the earth and subdue it;
Genesis 1:28

It has always been the intention of God that what is produced from you has the ability to fill the earth and subdue it. This is why you living in your house is the breeding ground for complacency. Because what is coming out of you consumes the environment it is around. Many of us were taught so wrong that Genesis will never actually make sense to us. You need to understand that verse like this contain massive amounts of revelation if you simply just read it. Because to imply that the earth was needing to be subdued by Adam, and his fruit would only indicate that it was not subdued at this time.

Which makes sense. Because you then understand that the Garden of Eden was not covering the earth. It was specific to one location, centrally located and bound by rivers in a place of God's choosing. And it was the intention of God that the thing He put in Adam had the ability to overtake the environment as he moved outside of that garden. It is also His intent that His plan could grow out of you and take over until what you were born in becomes the reality of what is around you.

The foundation of Christianity, whether we like to admit it or not, is not doctrine. I know that sounds heretical, but it's not. It's not a fundamental truth statement; it's not rituals or good works. It's not even a belief in Christ. James teaches us that demons believe also, and they tremble! (*James 2:19*). What separates Christianity from every other thought, religion, idea, cult, faction, or home group, is that the foundation of true Christianity is bearing fruit.

Luke 6:43-44
"For a good tree does not bear bad fruit, nor does a bad tree bear good fruit. For every tree is known by its own fruit."

But that really doesn't matter if it's winter. Because if the season dictates that *no one* is producing anything, then there is no pressure to really produce anything yourself. Understanding that the only difference between the living and the dead is what's on the inside toiling to come out. Think about it this way; a dead tree looks the same as a living tree in the winter. They both are brown, they both have limbs, they both have no leaves, and they both look dead. But on the inside of the living tree is millions of seed, dreams, plans, all waiting for the right season to let what is in it come out.

Most people love talking about what's coming because it excuses them for not having anything to show for what is here. I understand God is *wanting* to do something. That's pretty elementary, but what is He doing now? There must come a time in your walk when winter is over. And after winter comes spring time. And when springtime arrives, *the trees* that cannot produce fruit get really nervous because the environment around them begins to heat up.

And when nothing is inside of you, nothing will come out. Which is very frustrating because when nothing is coming out of you, then people who are bearing fruit will begin to look at you and wonder why you are not producing anything out of your life, when just a season ago, we were all in the same boat of unfruitfulness. But that was the winter. The springtime has a unique way of identifying who really is what they say they are.

> *"Let us learn to appreciate there will be times when the trees will be bare, and look forward to the time when we may pick the fruit."*
> *Anton Chekhov*

If there is one Kingdom principle that is grossly overlooked, and under-preached in the American church is the demand for fruit and good fruit at that.

We cannot continue to live uncommitted, inconsistent lives and call it Christianity. The Bible teaches us in Mark 16:17 that, "these **signs** will **follow** those who believe: In My name *they will* cast out demons; they will speak with new tongues;" So if signs are not following you, call it what you want but it does not qualify as believing! And even more disturbing to me is trying to wrap my brain around why in the world anyone would settle for sporadic church attendance at best when the potential is that signs would follow you? We have to understand what is expected of us and then burn to make it happen.

I have the great privilege afforded to me to be able to go to area churches on Sunday mornings and connect with other pastors, observe what The Lord is doing in other fellowships, etc. I am able to do this because our church does not gather together on Sunday mornings, but rather we have our community worship gathering on Sunday nights. With this opportunity I am able to witness the "watermark" of places.

Not from a judgmental standpoint, but as a self-evaluation standpoint. I want to see if other fellowships are doing something that we are missing. What I witness greatly disturbs me. For what I see is a group of people singing polished, practiced songs that *someone else wrote* to a God that is "far off" to them. I see form, not fire. I see the same exact thing that I saw growing up, except we've moved into rebellion in our clothing, dedication, convictions, etc. and labeled it as "freedom". I see Pastors striving to put forth some word of relevance, yet it lacks passion, and unveils the lack of spiritual devotion in the life of that Pastor. Not that all are that way, but almost all that I attend are.

I see pastors tilling ground that has been tilled entirely too much before. Preaching the same "revelation" as they preached ten years ago, singing the same songs, pretending to be Jenn Johnson, or Chris Tomlin, or whoever it is that pushes your worship team to be "modern". Using the same corny clichés, telling the same sad stories to get someone to feel emotional enough to respond to an altar call. There is no fruit, and where there is no fruit, people die.

"If you believe there is fruit that you know you should bear and do not, victory that you know you should have and have not, then I would say, 'Come on,' because God has something for you."

A.W. Tozer

We, as "clergy" (non-Biblical term that we adopted as sacred) preach against outward sins like adultery, fornication, alcoholism, tattoos, gambling, having long hair, wearing make-up, and whatever else it is that we are against, but very little demand fruit from their congregation. In over 20 years of ministry, this subject has caused more people to get offended with me (see previous chapter), and leave my church than any other topics combined, times two, squared, and rounded up. People hate for you to ask them what they are producing.

And people hate that because people are content with defining church as "that thing you do on Sunday as a part of your schedule." But Jesus set a much higher standard than church attendance, tipping of the offering plate, and a "good word" comment to the pastor as you're walking out the door to hurry home to catch the ball game, or get the boat in the water, or whatever else it is that you have on your "to-do" list.

I want to spring board this teaching from a story in Mark's gospel. Feel free to steal this and preach it yourself, but make sure you're producing it first.

Mark 11:12-14

And on the morrow, when they were come from Bethany, he was hungry: And seeing a fig tree afar off having leaves, he came, if haply he might find anything thereon: and when he came to it, he found nothing but leaves; for the time of figs was not yet. And Jesus answered and said unto it, No man eat fruit of thee hereafter forever. And his disciples heard it.

First let's take an exegetical look at what the writer is trying to convey through the power of the Holy Spirit. When he uses the phrase "On the Morrow", he is describing the idea of "Morning", or "A new day".

When reading scriptures, you must meditate and try to hear Holy Spirit whispering inside of the script. Because anytime we see the term, "new day" or synonyms thereof, it is indicative of the Christian salvation experience. It is literally a prophetic declaration of salvation, or being born again.

Revelation 21:5 says, "And he that sat upon the throne said, Behold, I make all things new." And Paul would teach us in 2 Corinthians 5:17 that "Therefore if any man be in Christ, he is a new creature: old things are passed away; behold, all things are become new." Likewise, in Psalm 30:5 we learn that "weeping may endure *for a night*, but joy cometh in the morning."

New days are important for the simple understanding that if they are new, they cannot be old. That's good right there! That means that there is literally no more reason to live in old ways. That regardless of what you could or could not accomplish yesterday, yesterday is gone, salvation is here! That is worth rejoicing over! That the old you is gone, and that today, there is new identity for you. That old habits die, and new ones are formed. That complacencies die. That fights and quarrels are buried with that old self. That depression can find someone else to bother, because that person you used to mess with doesn't live here anymore! This is the beauty of a new day.

And if it's new, it cannot be old. When you truly get born again, you begin a new day.

You receive new wine. And God then trusts you to know what to do with it. And when Jesus says that no one puts new wine in old wineskins, we tend to read that with an informal question to our tone of reading, but Jesus was stating a matter of fact. That if what you have is new, you DON'T put it into old lifestyle. It will not work. If what you have fits into your old lifestyle, then what you have isn't new. It may be emotional, it may be comforting to your compromising life, but it's not a new day. It's a shiny new penny, but it's still only a penny. We freak out over how shiny we can polish our compromise, and then sprinkle a little "greasy grace" on it by saying, "God understands".

NO HE DOESN'T.

I hate to make you uneasy right now, but understand that Jesus did everything He did on earth as a man, completely surrendered and submitted to God. He did it as a man, so that you and I could have a paradigm to base our walk on, and He did it so you and I could not have an excuse as to why we couldn't meet the mark. So, when we commit fornication, HE DOES NOT UNDERSTAND, because he was tempted in all ways as we are, and yet DID NOT SIN. He did everything He did *as a man* anointed of God so that you and I would be without excuse as to our laziness, and our inconsistency. You and I have the same Spirit as He did to come along side of you and help you. He chose to use you, you chose to not use it, and then ignorantly misuse a theological principle that He instituted and justify your inconsistency. No, if it fits in the old wineskin, it cannot be new wine.

Are You Hungry to see Fruit?

So, the story in Mark 11 tells us that "on the morrow, when they were come from Bethany, he was hungry…"

Jesus was hungry. Hunger is an interesting thing, especially in the Kingdom of God. Because in the earthly realm, you only get hungry when you don't eat. But in The Kingdom of God, the more you eat, the more hungry you become. And I believe that Jesus is just as hungry today to find fruit on those who claim to be connected to Him as He was that day. I believe the more fruit He gets a hold of in your life, the hungrier He gets to have more. His eyes are still burning with fire, looking for someone who is desperate to produce what they say they are. He's hungry to find fruit because fruit is a sign of the blessing. You not being able to produce anything is no different than the curse of the ground that was on Adam, and Cain, and Noah.

What in your life are you producing that is satisfying the hunger of Heaven?

Because what he's NOT looking for is all the things we think qualify us. He's not looking for intellectual stimulation. He's not looking for division in the name of man-made denominationalism. We do all that so we look good to ourselves and to each other. But if we cannot consume what you're producing, call it what you want, but it is NOT fruit! It may look like fruit on the outside, but I've seen a bowl full of fake fruit on a table that couldn't help anyone live. But it sure looked pretty.

We are forced to put labels on it, and we call it Christian on the sign out front, because if it weren't labeled, you wouldn't know what is inside. There is no fruit. We can dress the part, we can learn the cliché's and lingo, but if people walk in hungry, and cannot pick the fruit of your life and be satisfied, it's all just illegitimate. Because the beauty of hunger is that it forces you to begin to look for something that will satisfy that hunger. I know this first hand. Have you ever gotten up and walked to the fridge, opened the door, bent over a little, and just looked? You're not real sure what you want; you just know there's a gnawing inside of you for something. You're craving something to satisfy that uneasiness, that pain in your belly. Jesus was hungry, and His hunger drove him to look for something that had the ability to sustain him.

2 Chronicles 16:9 tells us, "For the eyes of the LORD run to and fro throughout the whole earth, to shew himself strong in the behalf of them whose heart is perfect toward him." Hunger pushes you to look for what will satisfy you. Listen church people, if hungry people are not hanging around you, you may to evaluate if the so called "fruit" is real or not.

I think Jesus is hungry, and He's looking at your tree.

I think He's really hungry

Don't buy the lie!

Mark 11:13
    And seeing a fig tree afar off *having leaves*, he came

    The danger of living in the curse is thinking you're doing well because you are growing. Leaves would indicate that the tree was healthy, and even more prophetically, it gives us insight into the fact that tree itself was growing. There is something we all learned in elementary school or middle school that most of us probably do not remember at all. It is a process called *photosynthesis*. This is a process where "the leaves collect energy from the sun and use it to manufacture sugars that *feed* the tree." It's grown enough to where it can feed itself!
    You growing to the point where you can sustain yourself and feed yourself is just the beginning of Christianity. And yet, sadly, we have made it the pinnacle. We have called consistent people things such as "mature", "pioneers", or even "Spiritual Giants". But the Bible calls consistent people things such as "disciple", "Christian", "pupil", "student", "son", "daughter". It is simply elementary to

produce what you are. An apple tree doesn't strive to produce apples. What it is comes out when it gets to the place of maturity.

Jesus didn't curse the tree for not growing. Weeds grow. The difference is that weeds don't produce fruit, *or* weeds don't produce "anything that can sustain the life of another"! The tree was growing fine. It knew how to feed itself. And that's good because God wants you to grow. But ultimately, if all you are doing is feeding yourself, you're not Kingdom, and even more disheartening is the true indication that you're not blessed.

Let me break it down for you "old school math class" style:

Jesus = the Kingdom = the Church = the body

If the body, the church, is not able to pull from what you are producing, you may be rock solid in your own growth, but *your job is not to grow, your job is to feed.*

John 21:17
He (Jesus) saith unto him (Peter) the third time, Simon, son of Jonas, lovest thou me? Peter was grieved because he said unto

him the third time, Lovest thou me? And he said unto him, Lord, thou knowest all things; thou knowest that I love thee. Jesus saith unto him, **Feed my sheep**.

If you love me, don't waste time telling me. Talk is cheap. If you love me, feed my sheep.

Are you producing fruit that sustains the body on its mission?

You do realize that Jesus was on a mission that day, and His plan and destiny was not to go visit and cruse a fig tree? He was on a mission and the fig tree was just where he passed by on the way to fulfill his mission. He was actually headed to be crucified! He had a purpose. He had a mission. And The Church also has a mission. The church of Jesus Christ also has a purpose, and your purpose is not to waste time walking around cursing things. Ask yourself this question, what could we be accomplishing if I was doing more than feeding myself? What if I was fueling the movement of the Body of Christ into the God ordained purpose?

You've got to realize that you were born for more than just getting old and dying comfortably! There's enough inside of you to fuel a ministry. There's enough inside of you to fuel a movement! And you're content with just leaves.

It's a growing tree. It's beautiful, it's strong, and it probably has a good root system (foundation). It has within itself the ability to live a long consistent life. So do you. But that wasn't its purpose. It was called a fig tree for one reason, and one reason only. Because it had the character of that which could produce figs. You see, existence and purpose are two different things. It could exist on its own. But its purpose for living was to bear fruit. As it stands, it's just a tree. We call it a fig tree, but it wasn't really a fig tree at this point, it was just a tree. Why? Because it didn't have any fruit to prove its identity.

You can tell the tree by the fruit that it bears.

"I'm a Christian". Are you? Or are you simply a morally decent human being? Because Christian is "in the likeness of Christ", and if you're not producing that fruit, you're a nice person, but nice people are not what we are called to become. You're entire existence and identity is wrapped not in your GIFT, but in your fruit. And **a gift that**

doesn't produce fruit is wasted seed, it's hypocrisy and SIN. You cannot have gifts of the spirit without producing fruit that can sustain the body. You being able to sing is not feeding the body, you picking up a 12 year old and spending time with him because he has no daddy is feeding the body! You getting a $5 carwash to help raise money for camp is not feeding the body. But you paying a kid's trip to summer camp, renting the van, and paying for the gas so that more kids can go *IS* feeding the kingdom.

So what is the curse?

The curse is that you continue to think you're good, and to think you're growing, and as long as you continue to be consistent, you're good. But the blessing is knowing that my identity is a "FIG" tree, and that is completely and solely based on the fact that when the body needs fruit, I can sustain it!

Mark 11: 20-23
And in the morning, as they passed by, they saw the fig tree *dried up from the roots*. And Peter calling to remembrance saith unto

him, Master, behold, the fig tree which thou cursedst is withered away. And Jesus answering saith unto them, Have faith in God. For verily I say unto you, That whosoever shall say unto this mountain, Be thou removed, and be thou cast into the sea; and shall not doubt in his heart, but shall believe that those things which he saith shall come to pass; he shall have whatsoever he saith.

Don't miss this. The tree was rooted in, yet it was dry. This is so pivotal in understanding the curse of unfruitfulness that Jesus explains the dryness of this little fig tree with the analogy of a mountain. He tells them "Whoever shall say unto this mountain."

What mountain?

It's a tree?

I believe Jesus used the analogy of a mountain because the mountain speaks prophetically of you living under the curse that accepts your identity in your self-sufficiency and not in your ability to feed others. This thing is much bigger than you think it is, but the good news, is that if you have faith, you can remove this hindrance in your life and you can start producing fruit than remains!

Chapter 5:

The Blessing of appropriated honor

"Honor is like an island, rugged and without shores; once we have left it, we can never return."
Nicolas Boileau

Okay, let's say for a moment that you have connected with what we have been learning so far. Most people are right there with me until we get to this subject. But I have found through experience the greatest blessings that I have in my life are the product of appropriating honor where honor was due, and stewarding over that correctly.

I have a friend who is a massive voice in this country. His name is Bryn Waddell. He walks in such amazing blessing because he understands the power of appropriated honor. He was recently at our church and spoke briefly about the concept of honor:

"Honor is not about the person. Honor is about seeing the God on the person. Honor is giving proper due to the portion of God that is upon a man or woman. Our generation hates it because we have seen people overemphasis people worship, and so now we think everybody is our homeboy. No, everybody is not our homeboy. There are men and women who carry more weight than we. We may not like it, it may offend us because we don't want to think that somebody is better in God than we are, but it's not about that, it's about gifting, calling, and weight in the Kingdom of God. And **there are men and women who carry more weight than you and I. And our response to that should be honor**. It should not be distain, it should not be *'oh whatever'*, it should not be *'oh they think they're high and mighty'*;

No, they're who God called them to be, and you can either deal with it or not deal with it, but it's still up to you to honor the portion of the presence of God on a man or woman that you see as that thing. We don't understand this, but honor is an 'unlocker'. Honor unlocks the giftings, the anointings and portion of the presence of God in the life of another and allows you to receive it. Because your ability to receive is based on and consistent with your level to perceive. If you receive a prophet in the name of the prophet, you receive the prophet's reward. So, if you receive a prophet as just *'some dude'*, or *'some guy that's just my homey'*, you are going to get the *'homey'* reward. Our generation does not understand this. Because Jesus is *'our homeboy'*, and *everybody's cool, everybody's on the same level*. Everyone is NOT on the same playing field. There are people that carry more weight, and you have to just deal with that."

Wow! This is such a powerful word of putting into clarity the necessity for appropriated honor. And there is massive blessing attached to appropriating honor to those God has placed in your life as spiritual leaders. And since the opposite of the blessing is the curse, we can rightly conclude that if we are not appropriating honor correctly, we are trying to produce inside of a curse. And that just does not work. Let me show you what I mean.

Genesis 18:9-12 NKJV
Then they said to him, "Where *is* Sarah your wife?" So he said, "Here, in the tent." And He said, "I will certainly return to you according to the time of life, and behold, Sarah your wife shall have a son." (Sarah was listening in the tent door which *was* behind

him.) Now Abraham and Sarah were old, well advanced in age; *and* Sarah had passed the age of childbearing. Therefore Sarah laughed within herself, saying, "After I have grown old, shall I have pleasure, my lord being old also?"

Pretty familiar scripture to most of us, but I want to first deal with the greatest hindrance we have to appropriating honor. Because if we deal with this in your life, we can unlock blessing like never before. Most of us feel as though we need explanation, understanding, and must be in agreement before we release honor. But there is no submission until we reach the point of disagreement, and you chose to walk in the instruction of the one appointed to be above you, rather than walk in your own *'understanding'*.

I have had numerous people follow my vision, and honor me, and submit to my guidance right up until the point where I saw something in their life that they didn't see, or didn't want to deal with, and immediately, they jumped ship. And today, without exception, they are living in a sinful, backslidden state. I do not know of one single person who is progressing spiritually since that time of disagreement, and them choosing to walk away. That's not honor. That's picking which ride you want to go on at the county fair. That's juvenile, spoiled, arrogant, prideful, and anti-Christ.

The idea that you are given the right to understand, or the right of preference, or the right to have a disagreeing opinion has been one of the greatest fuels to keep us all under the curse. What screams loudly as the dominant difference between the life of Adam and Eve and the life of Abraham is that Adam and Eve were deceived by their lack of trust due to their sense of entitlement. They felt as though their confusion or "misguidedness" as to God's intent was excuse enough to go against the word of God. In other words, they were saying, "I don't see the big deal, and since I don't see the big deal, there's not a big deal." This sounds eerily familiar to me.

But Abraham comes on the scene and we see a life that is consistent in trust and agreement with the word of the Lord. Imagine if you're Abraham, with no Bible, no church, living out in the desert, worshipping rocks, and the moon, and lizards, and whatever else he was doing, and you hear the word of the Lord saying, "Leave your home; Leave your country; Leave your family; Go to a land that I WILL SHOW YOU EVENTUALLY." That's pretty insane to me. Then, when he's really, really old, the word of the Lord says to him, "Look into the sky and number the stars, these are your descendants." Nothing inside of Abraham had the capacity to agree with that statement. Literally.

But what separates us from Abraham is the same issue as we see with Adam and Eve, and with many others. Abraham never questioned God due to lack of understanding. He never said, *"hey God, I don't think so, I thought it would be easier than this, so I'm just gonna step back into where I was"*. Abraham believed God with no explanation, no understanding, nothing. And we hardly ever believe anything until we understand and see the value of the return before the investment. And for some reason, we label that as faith. I don't think that's what it is called.

What fuels the curse of toil and unfruitfulness in our lives is the fact that we feel that we deserve the privilege of understanding before we walk in obedience, and honor. That is a doctrine created in America, for Americans to excuse them from living the Bible's standards. Because nowhere in the Bible is the theology of *"understanding before honoring and obeying."* You don't get that privilege. Most all of us feel we deserve the right to understand and even worse than that, we feel we have the right to voice our opinion. You don't. Unless you're okay walking in the curse, and not walking in blessing. Because if that's the case, build yourself a website and blog until your fingers bleed about your opinion, but at the end of the day, I want to walk in blessing.

It starts with a change of thinking.

Most people have the attitude that honor is what you get before you give. If that's you, you will, without a doubt, continue to be the lone wolf wanderer. You will always be the one who stirs a lot of noise but it's just noise because it's not blessed. You'll have a lot of stories about what God is doing in YOU, which is unbiblical, because after the resurrection of Jesus, he established his church, not his lone wolf. And you'll spend your whole life dropping little fire crackers that get people's attention for a second, but there's nothing after the bang. I know too many people who are a "giant rock" in their own mind, but won't ever be able to fill a gap in the wall because they'd rather be a big rock alone, than to be chiseled on to where the fit in the gap. We don't need you. Go somewhere else!

You may not think you need spiritual authority in your life, and if that's you, let the record show that it was God that established this divine order, and whether you agree with it or not, you get in the order or else you walk in the curse.

Ephesians 4:11-13 NKJV
    And He Himself gave some *to be* apostles, some prophets, some evangelists, and some pastors and teachers, for the equipping of the saints for the work of ministry, for the edifying of the body of Christ, till we all come to the unity of the faith and of the knowledge of the Son of God, to a perfect man, to the measure of the stature of the fullness of Christ;

You should really read your Bible.

It is through submission and appropriated honor that we are permitted to come into unity of faith. Seriously, you should read your Bible. Because then, and only then, are we positioned to become what the Bible calls "a perfect man". When you begin to place appropriated honor on spiritual authority and truly follow that vision, you step into the blessing attached to that person.

Hebrews 13:17 KJV

Obey them that have the rule over you, and submit yourselves: for they watch for your souls, as they that must give account, that they may do it with joy, and not with grief: **for that is unprofitable for you.**

And this is far more than obedience. Obedience is the elementary standard. Honor and obedience look identical on the outside. Just the same as holiness and legalism look the same on the outside. Meaning that two different people can serve by cleaning the church and one is doing it because it was asked of them. The other is because they honor the authority over them. One will receive a blessing, while the other will continue to wear the chains of slavery because your heart and mind are not appropriating the correct honor to the person over you. Because what they do may look the same, but in time, the fruit of the blessing of appropriated honor will begin to show in one life, while the other will do like most of us do, and get frustrated that we are not seeing results when we are *"doing what we're supposed to do"*.

Obedience is done out of respect for authority and their position. For example, you do what you're told to do at your job because if you don't, the person who told you to do it has the power to remove you from that job. However, the blessing of appropriated honor is produced through you believing *in the person* leading you to the point where even if you do not have faith in their decisions, that even if you do not have understanding in why they chose to lead the way they do, that even in spite of any of that, you submit your will to theirs.

You don't bring dishonor to the leader that God put you under. Your "need to understand why" is not an excuse to bring dishonor to the institution of His church and worse, it's not an excuse to continue to see your life be unfruitful, and you continue to raise your children under that curse.

So what is the blessing of appropriated honor?

Let's look at how this works out for dear Sarah. First off, understand that Sarah didn't just have small faith, Sarah had anti-faith. We conclude this because the Bible tells us that she laughed within herself. She literally sucked all the faith out of the room. Do you know people like that? Maybe you are the person? That when God opens a door for you to appropriate honor, you laugh within yourself because you are looking at the functionality of the vessel He's choosing to use to pour that blessing on you with? Sarah has anti-faith, and the reason she has anti-faith is because she looked at the situation and realized that within herself, she had no ability to produce it, and her husband had no ability to produce it.

And this seems almost "anti the nature of God" because we find her receiving the blessing of Abraham with anti-faith. This screams out in me to not be fair. How is it that God is pouring out blessing on Sarah with anti-faith? The answer is that Sarah, although she has no faith in the word, appropriates honor on Abraham, and we know this because of one small phrase in the next verse of the story.

Verse 12 again
Therefore Sarah laughed within herself, saying, "After I have grown old, shall I have pleasure, *my lord* being old also?"

Did you catch it? She calls Abraham her Lord. Wow! This was Sarah, with anti-faith, showing appropriated honor and submission to the spiritual authority over her, and it caused her to walk in the blessing! Not only did she break the curse of barrenness, but by appropriated honor, she gained access to all that Abraham had, including HIS FAITH. I understand that to some, it borders heresy to say this, but in this story, she didn't need faith, she needed to just submit, and trust, without understanding. The blessing of honor and submission is that even if you do not understand or even if you lack certain things, you receive by default of position, based on your honor. Let me give you another example:

2 Kings 13:4
Now Elisha was fallen sick of his sickness whereof he died. And Joash the king of Israel

came down unto him, and wept over his face, and said, O my father, my father, the chariot of Israel, and the horsemen thereof.

Elisha, the prophet, is on his deathbed. King Joash comes to the mighty miracle worker, and voice of God for the nation, knowing that no one has made the effort to position themselves to inherit his mantle. He approaches the man of God, and uses the term "father" when addressing Elisha. Now, we skip through this, but understand that Joash has not ever served Elisha, he has never traveled with him, he has never followed him from place to place. Joash never took time to study prophetic ministry. He didn't have seminary papers, he didn't walk up to him and say, "Prophet, prophet", and he didn't say "Master, Master". No, he comes to the mighty man of God and calls him "father", and that appropriated honor caused Elisha to be willing to release his double portion over him because of his willingness to submit and honor the man of God.

God has a plan for Abraham, but that plan includes Sarah. And God has a plan for your church, and the plan includes you. God has a plan for your city and the plan includes you.

God has a plan for you, and that plan includes those who are around you, coming along side of you and helping you accomplish the vision God gave you!

"There must be cooperation with God's plan. Isaac was not immaculately conceived."
Bill Johnson

Many times God will allow you to be put into a position that will test you. Not just for YOUR destiny, but to connect you to other destinies. Why would God do this? He does this in order to show you how big the picture needs a lot of small puzzle pieces to make the whole. Get this in your head. Abraham's promise is not possible without Sarah, and she has anti-faith. SELAH. She actually has faith in the impossibility of God's word. But so did Moses. So did Gideon. So did the Disciples on numerous occasions. We call Abraham the father of our faith, but do you know Sarah gets ALL the credit for being the mother of our faith? How is it that the mother of our faith had no faith? How did she come into that position? She is the mother of our faith simply because she had correctly placed honor on her head-covering, and in spite of what she thought, she inherited all that he had. We know this because in unity, two become one. And inside of that union, where one part is lacking, the fulfillment of it is found in the other.

Amos 3:3
      Can two walk together, unless they are agreed?

Another way of looking at this union is to say, "My lack in compassion is made up for by my wife's excess in compassion." So I am compassionate by default, not by faith, but by appropriated honor of her. The same is true in the opposite, that her lacks are made up for by my strengths. So that if she is in lack, I will cover it.

Very few people who connect to a body of believers have not had a moment of disagreement with how the church is being run. Opinions and disagreements on trivial things like decorations, who gets to play Jesus in the Easter cantata? Where does all the money go? (For most it stays in your pockets). Why is the music so loud? Why is always so cold in here? Why is it always hot in here? And people will quit going to a church for the silliest of reasons. And what all the devils in hell want you to do, is to continue to read your Bible, and continue to pray, and continue to go to church, and continue to feel privileged, and to continue to feel like your opinion counts. And to continue to feel like we have to cater to you, because as long as you keep thinking that, all of the praying and reading and effort you are making is for naught.

As long as you keep thinking that way, you will continue to walk in the curse, and even worse, you will continue to hinder the body from walking in the "unity of faith" until we come to a perfect man. Being an Apostolic ministry (and some may not understand that term) means that you're going to see all aspects of my life that are not "*third Heaven holy*". You're going to see my good attributes, but you will also see some of my bad ones. I was taught, as was an entire generation, that you don't get close to your people because you don't want them to get to know you too well, or they won't honor and respect you and they'll see your flaws.

But can you handle knowing your pastor is not perfect and still honor the house God has placed you in? Can you still push for the vision to be completed? Can you keep your mouth shut when you don't understand or don't get your way? God will place you in the institution of His church, and under true apostolic covering and expose you to their imperfections, and then force you to honor them, in order to receive the blessing. And when you are asked about the person or situation you are in, God will force you to paint that picture with honor. And keep your opinions to yourself.

Listen, ministers will hurt you and break your heart, and you will have to honor and say, they are a wonderful man of God, and truly mean it. We do not know how to do that. And because we do not know how to do that, we continue to walk in the curse attached to it.

> *"Honor is only honor in the presence of imperfection."*
> Casey Doss

If the pastor was perfect and you honored them, it would not be honor, it would be common sense. But God will show you all the imperfections of what you're "married to" and then test you to see if you can still honor them and received from them even if you truly don't know or believe what they are doing may be right, in your opinion. If you can learn honor, you can walk in the blessing of unity, of the perfect man, even if your faith is not up to par. And you can inherit everything you lack.

So do this, go submit to your pastor. Ask him/her to write out their vision for the house, and where they see you fitting into that vision, and then do whatever they say with a heart that says, I want to honor them so that I walk in the blessings of God for my life! If it's available for me, I want it. This may mean that you are the newest cleaner of toilets in your church. If that's the case, you scrub it with all your heart, knowing a mantle of blessing is your reward!

Exodus 20:12
"Honor your father and your mother, so that you may live long in the land the LORD your God is giving you."

Old timers used to say this is because if you don't honor them, they'll take you out! God blesses you when you pour honor on people!

Chapter 6:

The Curse of Robbing God

A gift opens doors; it gives access to the great.
Proverbs 18:16

This is where most people stop reading, stop listening, close their books, and tell people that the book was *good until he started talking about money*. But people only get upset when you start pulling on things rooted deep in them. If any of the men out there have ever had a pesky nose hair then you understand what I am talking about. You grasp those tweezers with the compounded strength of a dozen Clydesdales. Close one eye to get proper depth perception and accuracy of target approach. You grab gently, and then wiggle ever so slightly to ensure that you got a sure grip on that one little bothersome hair, and then, knowing the pain you are about to invoke upon yourself, with all your might, you yank quickly, hoping to have a clean removal.

And then, after the tears have clouded your vision, and you sniff a few times, you look into the mirror, only to find that the tiny little lonely hair has roots that reach all the way down to your little toe. Because it only hurts when it's rooted deep in you and money is what most people have a problem with hearing anything about, especially from preachers.

So, before you cast your stones, and put the book down, remember the purpose of this reading is to get you from walking under a curse into walking in every possible blessing available throughout the Holy Scriptures. And besides, don't you want to fund the Kingdom? Guess what? Your Heavenly Father wants you to do the same.

Perversion feeds the curse

Because we don't pay the price to properly understand revelation, we quickly accept a perverted version of other people's revelation. Let me show you what I mean by that. Prosperity is Biblical. Isn't it? Is prosperity Biblical? Do you even know? What verse do you know that says that? The reality is that Prosperity is Biblical, and we will prove that with Scripture later in this chapter, but for now, trust me that prosperity is Biblical. However, there have been men and women who claim to speak and hear from God who have not paid the price to properly understand prosperity, and they abuse the word of God in order to manipulate people out of money. This is not right at all, but it does not negate the fact that prosperity is of God, and it is a means by which He shows Himself strong in your life. But perversion has caused people to develop a mentality that says, "All the church wants is our money so that fat preacher can get fatter." (Paraphrased and strongly opinionated, of course, but you get the idea).

And so what happens? Some innocent, yet ignorant preachers have developed such a fear of being seen as *"one of those kind of preachers"*, that they swing the pendulum completely to the other side, and preach that God is only truly glorified when you are poor. And neither of which are the true Biblical doctrine or revelation of prosperity.

Let me give you another. Now, we would all probably agree that wives submitting to husbands is Biblical. However, some people, who are not willing to dig into the word themselves, and hear from God, begin to manipulate that blessing into a controlling spirit, and they use it to literally belittle and abuse women. That is nothing as to what the Word of God intended for this scripture to be used for. And since some people didn't want to be labeled as "that guy", they go the opposite direction and teach that women don't have to submit at all. Again, neither are right. So, regardless of the perversion, ma'am, you still have to submit to your husband, like it or not. And if you had a revelation of its purpose, you would love it! Because your husband still has to love you like Christ loved the church. And how did He love the Church?

Most everyone responds with *"He died for it."* And I would agree that He did die for the Church, but that has NOTHING to do with this scripture. Christ loved the Church by giving up His purpose at the right hand of the Father in Heaven, and giving up His position, so that He could put ALL HIS EFFORT into making *HER* (The Bride's) purpose possible. Ladies, it's easy to submit to a husband whose life's purpose is to lay his dreams down to make sure your purpose is fulfilled. We don't like to talk about that in the church, but it's doctrine, like it or not!

When we start talking about giving, and money, and where you put your investments and people go straight to the perversions. As a matter of fact, I was so confused by this perversion that when we started our church many years ago, we didn't take up the first offering until three months into it.

But Giving is AS BIBLICALLY a Command as praying and fasting according to Jesus, and just as spiritual.

Malachi 3: 6-18

"For I *am* the LORD, I do not change; Therefore you are not consumed, O sons of Jacob. Yet from the days of your fathers you have gone away from my ordinances and have not kept *them*. Return to Me, and I will return to you," says the LORD of hosts. "But you said, 'In what way shall we return?' "Will a man rob God? Yet you have robbed Me! But you say, 'In what way have we robbed You?' In tithes and offerings. You are cursed with a curse, For you have robbed Me, *even* this whole nation. Bring all the tithes into the storehouse, that there may be food in My house, and try Me now in this," says the LORD of hosts, "If I will not open for you the windows of heaven and pour out for you *such* blessing that *there will* not *be room* enough *to receive it*. "And I will rebuke the devourer for your sakes, so that he will not destroy the fruit of your ground, nor shall the vine fail to bear fruit for you in the field," says the LORD of hosts; "And all nations will call you blessed, for you will be a delightful land," says the LORD of hosts. "Your words have been harsh against Me," Says the LORD, "Yet you say, 'What have we spoken against You?' You have said, 'It is useless to serve God; what profit *is it* that we have kept His ordinance, and that we have walked as mourners before the LORD of hosts? So now we call the proud blessed, for those who do wickedness are raised up;

They even tempt God and go free.'" Then those who feared the LORD spoke to one another, and the LORD listened and heard them; So a book of remembrance was written before Him for those who fear the LORD and who meditate on His name. "They shall be Mine," says the LORD of hosts, "On the day that I make them My jewels. And I will spare them as a man spares his own son who serves him." Then you shall again discern between the righteous and the wicked, between one who serves God and one who does not serve Him.

In Verse 7, Where God tells them, "Return to me, and I will return to you." We see that their response is, "In what way shall we return?" This little exchange of words is the devastating result of living in the curse of robbing God. There are many times in our lives where we think our questions, or our actions are innocent, and that God just overlooks us because we are ignorant little children. But *our ignorance is only fruit of our lack of investment in getting to know Him*. When they say, "In what way shall we return?"

They are revealing that their mentality was, "We didn't know we had left". Showing us something deeply detrimental to your growth as a Christian. That when you hold back your tithe AND offering, you are spiritually walking away from Him, and most will not even know they have walked away. Now, understand something, this is NEVER preached this way, but it's scriptural. It is perverted and preached that *God won't bless you if you don't give your money*. That's just not true.

The curse attached to withholding tithe and offerings is that you are walking away from God while your feet never move. It is a subtle walk. You don't even recognize that it's happening. It is holding you back from growth, it is childish, it is elementary and it is sin.

In Fact, Paul teaches us that giving is a sign of maturing faith. In Romans 12:3-8, he says, " For I say, through the grace given to me, to everyone who is among you, not to think *of himself* more highly than he ought to think, but to think soberly, as God has dealt to each one *a measure of faith.* For as we have many members in one body, but all the members do not have the same function, so we, *being* many, are one body in Christ, and individually members of one another. Having then gifts differing **according to the grace that is given to us,** *let us use them:* if prophecy, *let us prophesy* in proportion to our faith; or ministry, *let us use it* in *our* ministering; he who teaches, in teaching; he who exhorts, in exhortation; <u>**he who gives, with liberality**</u>; he who leads, with diligence; he who shows mercy, with cheerfulness.

In the last Chapter we talked about honor. That Hebrews 13:17 says, " Obey them that have the rule over you, and submit yourselves: for they watch for your souls, as they that must give account, that they may do it with joy, and not with grief: for **that is**

unprofitable for you." Obedience is a wonderful thing, but honor is required for blessing. We have taught out of Malachi as a mandate, and a rule, looking like it's a switch we flip by obedience, and we know obedience IS BETTER than sacrifice. But that is simply the elementary understanding of what is being taught here. Because the blessing of honor is doing what you do because you love the one you do it for, not because you're told to.

Matthew 6:31-34

"So don't worry about these things, saying, 'What will we eat? What will we drink? What will we wear?' *These things dominate the thoughts of unbelievers*, but your heavenly Father already knows all your needs. Seek the Kingdom of God above all else, and live righteously, and he will give you everything you need. "So don't worry about tomorrow, for tomorrow will bring its own worries. Today's trouble is enough for today."

Tithing is a response of obedience, while an offering is a response of trust, and the fruit of both is walking in blessing.

So, let's look at some Biblical guidelines for tithe, *and for offerings*, and pray that it challenges you to honor God where it really counts.

"The Almighty Dollar"

Why is money such a big issue? The truth is that it's only big to you. Money is not a big issue to God, but it is to us. It's a big deal to us because, whether we admit it or not, it is your true provider, and it is your true security. I know people, and I'm sure that you do too, that when you think of them, every attribute of them is wrapped in how much money they have, from their vehicles, to houses, to the way they talk; Their god is their money, and their money is their god.

And they may tithe, and may even give offerings, but they are giving out of obligation because there is no fruit of blessing attached to it anywhere in their life. You have to get beyond the trivial thinking that cars and nice houses are "The blessings" of God. While they do fall under that category, they do not define it. If they did, then poor people living in third world countries could never be blessed. We have to break this materialist mindset.

Matthew 6:24

"No one can serve two masters; for either he will hate the one and love the other, or else he will be loyal to the one and despise the other. You cannot serve God and mammon (money).

"The Tithe"

In 1 Chronicles 29:1-20 David gives a tremendous offering, and he calls Israel to give. Most scholars have estimated that they, as a whole gave 190 tons of gold, 375 tons of silver, 675 tons of bronze, and 3750 tons of iron.

Leviticus 27:30-31

"One-tenth of the produce of the land, whether grain from the fields or fruit from the trees, belongs to the LORD and must be set apart to him as holy. If you want to buy back the LORD's tenth of the grain or fruit, you must pay its value, plus 20 percent.

A better understanding of how that applies today is that **if you miss an opportunity to give tithe**, and keep it, that you **not only pay it back next time, but add 20%.** Some of you just threw this book across the room and called me a false prophet. That's okay, it's not me saying it, this is the Word of God. It's a tenth if you give it. But if you want to keep it, it's a tenth, plus 20% to get back in right standing, and keep the devourer away. That hurts to even read doesn't it? How many of you can readily admit that there are times you've not given your tithe? You have just set yourself up to walk away from the Lord without even knowing it, and the step to get back where you are is to return and pay what you missed and add 20%. **We do not do this**! But if we did, we would walk in such favor and blessing, because God would see that money is simply a tool He's given us to sing the Kingdom song!

What exactly is *The Tithe*?

The word "tithe" simply means "one tenth" of something. When you understand that this was not just a term used in Church settings to describe the portion you give to the church, but it is far more than that. In the Old Testament God commanded Israel to give a tithe of everything that they owned. One-tenth of their produce, one-tenth of their land, one-tenth of their belongings. This is a gross difference to what we qualify as a tithe. As a matter of fact, what we give is far less than a tithe, even though it may be a tenth of the finances we have coming into our house. **The tithe was a "Set aside portion" of EVERYTHING that came into your house.** So, here we are in the world we live in having serious debates and even church splits over some things as asinine and mindless as *should I tithe on the gross or net income?* Or even debates like *should I tithe on my tax return?* My answer to people for any and all of these questions is simply this: **"Did it COME IN TO your house?"** If the answer is yes, then God expects the tithe, according to the Old Testament. And then I usually say something to offend them like, "If this is still an issue for you, then you are probably not doing it right anyway, and it won't be blessed, so give whatever."

A picture of the REAL tithe

In The Old Testament, the tithe was only taken once a year, not every meeting as we in today's society. And the yearly tithe was taken to turn around and supply the needs for three different divisions:

First of all, a tithe (one-tenth of everything that they came into possession of) went to the wellbeing and taking care of the Levitical priests. Remember, the Levites received no inheritance of land, so they had to strictly trust the Lord to cause the people of the land to provide for them, while they performed their priestly duties for those same people. That can be found in Numbers 18:21-24.

Secondly, a yearly tithe was collected (that's another ten percent of whatever came into their household) in order to provide for community celebration. Scriptural proof for this is found in Deuteronomy 12:17-18, and also in Deuteronomy 14:22-23.

Thirdly, and this only happened every third year, but on the third year, a third tithe was collected (that's ten more percent, on top of the twenty percent they have already given). This tithe was collected to help poor and needy of the community. It was to meet the needs of the orphans and the widows, and those who could not provide for themselves.

This can be found in Deuteronomy 14:28-29, and also in Deuteronomy 26:12-13.

Let's make sure you understand this. Those three categories of tithing were not the same, but three different tithe. Three different offerings that were each consisting of one-tenth of everything that came into their house throughout the year. **It WAS NOT a tenth split three ways.** It was one-tenth that was required three times. First, a tenth for the priests required once a year, second, for celebrations, given once a year. And thirdly, for orphans and widows, once every three years.

And if you are somewhat decent at math, you would conclude that each year, the Israelites were required by God to give 23.33% of their income. Do you see this? That the bare minimum that the Bible required for Israel in order to properly represent their covenant with God was 23% of their yearly income. And God instituted a way for them to give in accordance to what they had; out of everything they owned.

Now, in the scripture I referenced earlier, the millions of tons that were given to the temple by David, and the people of God was in addition to, and on top of their 23% required! Do you see this? That they had so stewarded correctly over what they had, and gave according to their income, and increase, that God so richly blessed all of them, that when the King asked for an offering, there was literal tons of money given. That's the blessing of the tithe. You cannot out-give God!

To borrow some statistics from the website, Daveramsey.com (December 2008)*"Americans who earn less than $10,000 gave 2.3 percent of their income to religious organizations, whereas those who earn $70,000 or more gave only 1.2 percent." While the actual percentages are slightly higher for Christians who regularly attend church, the pattern is similar. Households of committed Christians making less than $12,500 per year give away roughly 7 percent of their income, a figure no other income bracket beats until incomes rise above $90,000 (they give away 8.8 percent).*

"If members of historically Christian churches in the United States had raised their giving to the

Old Testament's minimum standard of giving (10% of income) in 2000, **an additional $139,000,000,000** *a year would become available assist in Christian based mission work."*

And that is JUST the Old Testament tithe.

"If you've been saved more than a year, and all you give is your tithe, you need to wake up."
Damon Thompson

Offerings:

Tithing was an Old Testament command from God. Giving an offering is a New Testament command from Jesus. And it's not optional.

Matthew 6:2 says, "**When** you give to someone in need…"

Giving is the only excess God will not cause you to stumble because of! You cannot "out give" Him!

"He is rich or poor according to what he is, not according to what he has." – Henry Ward Beecher

God's plan is not that you have a poverty spirit. A person who is bound with a poverty spirit always feels like their resources are limited. But God never intended for us to live in poverty in any area of our lives! Not one area. We are His sons and daughters! However, He does want us to be good stewards over what he has given us, so he won't be wasting good seed on us because we're not responsible. David said, "I have been young, and now I am old, and I have never seen the righteous forsaken, or his descendants begging for bread." (Psalm 37:25). David was qualified to say this because he had positioned himself as a giver.

Giving is a matter of care towards someone, not how much you have available.

Before our church broke into this amazing revival that we are in currently, God began to show me what it meant to be a giver. Four years before the revival started, I was led of Holy Spirit to begin supporting a ministry not in my city, or even my county, but on the far side of the state. But I knew I had to partner with them, because I wanted the revival they were in to visit our little town. I committed to giving $100 a month to them. That was tremendously hard. At times it felt as though I was throwing away $100. At times we needed to get groceries, or my children needed something for school, and when your kids' needs are what you balancing your giving against, it's very difficult to follow God in that moment. But I did. For four years, I gave $100 a month, and today I still give $100 a month, but what happened was that God honored my heart of giving above what was asked of me by the law, and he sent the revival that we prayed and fasted and longed for. But I believe that the door to Heaven was unlocked because I was willing to give above my tithe, to a field I would not yield any harvest from, only to receive all the blessing of that field simply from my obedience, and my love for His will.

"The doorway to breaking the spirit of poverty is giving"

Karen Wheaton

Can I just stop here and tell you how much I love Karen Wheaton. Never in my life have I witnessed such a driven, blessed, anointed servant of God. Find her online and write her a check today!

> "Abram *was* very rich in livestock,
> in silver, and in gold."
> Genesis 13:2

The thing that we all love about tithing is that it is specific and proportionate to our income. Specific to what we get from our jobs, or from other people. Tithing is safe for us because it paints the bare minimum, and we are okay giving the bare minimum. We like it because we know how much we "have" to give.

Which, ironically, is the exact same attribute that we despise about the concept of giving an offering. Giving an offering is NOT proportionate to our income; it is done strictly out of our heart's overflow and our good stewardship. And if done correctly, we are permitted to give more, and more. And that scares us because we love our money going to us.

Giving offerings demonstrates love, not law

Giving offerings was a biblical command that was not specified or limited by amount, size, value, quality or purpose. Giving offerings was done to *show honor* to people. We learn in 2 Samuel 8:2 that "the Moabites became David's servants, *and* brought him tribute". We also read in Daniel 2:48 that, "the king promoted Daniel and gave him many great gifts". Giving offerings was also done as a means of celebration. Revelation 11:10 says, "And those who dwell on the earth will rejoice over them, make merry, and send gifts to one another".

Amy Carmichael once said, "You can give without loving, but you cannot love without giving." Listen, you are never more like God than when we give! Mark 12:41-44 says, "Jesus sat down near the collection box in the Temple and watched as the crowds dropped in their money. Many rich people put in large amounts.
Then a poor widow came and dropped in two small coins. Jesus called his disciples to him and said, "I tell you the truth, this poor widow has given more than all the others who are making contributions. For they gave a tiny

part of their surplus, but she, poor as she is, has given everything she had to live on."

A man is not measured by what he has, but by what has him. Some people own houses, and some people, their houses own them. Because there is a huge difference between being rich and being wealthy. Wealthy people refuse to be reduced by their balance sheet and their wealth never has them. But rich people's self-esteem is attached directly to their "profit and loss" statement.

Giving offerings is directly related to how well we manage the remainder of our money. You cannot pay God to be your money manager. It does not work that way. Giving does not "force" God to bless you. What giving an offering above your tithe does is that it forces YOU to be a good steward over the rest of what you do have. It forces self-control. It forces taking inventory and not just flippantly spending whatever you want on whatever you want. If you want increase, you need to understand that it is directly tied to proper management of what you do have.

One thing I have learned, and it has helped me tremendously, is to use the internet to my advantage when it comes to spending money. Let me explain. When I am out at a store, and I see something I need, and sometimes it's just something I want, I pull out my smart phone and use it for something besides twitter updates, snapchats, selfies, or taking pictures of random people dressed like they forgot they were leaving their house to actually go out in public. Instead, I look the item up on certain shopping apps (take your pick).

If I can find it cheaper, I order it there. I am willing to wait the extra three days for it to ship to my house, than to spend the extra amount of money in order to have it today. *"Patience young padawan; I will teach you the way!"* Patience is vital, especially if it is not a necessity. I have another rule when shopping. If what you pick up is not cheaper online, it is also not a necessity, but a luxury; if it is something you don't really need, but you want, do this, put it in your buggy, and then walk around the store for ten more minutes not picking anything else up. Just walk and look and wrestle in your mind with the idea that you really don't need to spend the money for this. 24 out of 25 times you will put it back on the shelf. It works!

2 Corinthians 9:6-12 NKJV

But this *I say:* He who sows sparingly will also reap sparingly, and he who sows bountifully will also reap bountifully. *So let* each one *give* as he purposes in his heart, not grudgingly or of necessity; for God loves a cheerful giver. And God *is* able to make all grace abound toward you, that you, always having all sufficiency in all *things,* may have an abundance for every good work. As it is written: "He has dispersed abroad, He has given to the poor; His righteousness endures forever." Now may He who supplies seed to the sower, and bread for food, supply and multiply the seed you have *sown* and increase the fruits of your righteousness, while *you are* enriched in everything for all liberality, which causes thanksgiving through us to God. For the administration of this service not only supplies the needs of the saints, but also is abounding through many thanksgivings to God."

Verse 7 teaches us to give not out of necessity, do not give out of it being required of you. Not out of obedience to the call, but give from the heart. Righteous giving is done from the righteous heart, not a legalistic quota. I have three goals (challenges) I submit to you to strive to achieve, and there is no time limit on this, so set them as a daily reminder somewhere you see often (the refrigerator, bathroom, next to the TV remote). These goals are lifelong goals, character goals, and they do not end.

"The Blessed Giver" Goals:

1 – Give an offering EVERY TIME I'm asked. If you have to post-date a check because McDonalds won the fight all week, determine to be a giver EVERY TIME.

2 – Consider my stewardship so that I will have more to give to the Kingdom. I have set myself to get my finances in order to the point where I can one day give at least 50% of my income. That's my goal. Why? Because I want to have such a large foundation built that God

can release his "unheard of" blessing over it.

3 – I will start looking for needs in my community and if I can, I will meet the need myself. I do this. Especially in the summer time. I load my yard equipment up and I drive through random neighborhoods looking for tall grass, and if I see a yard, I stop, get out and cut it. I don't knock on the door, I don't ask permission. I give!

Make these goals character traits of your life and watch the blessings flow! Because *the hand that gives, gathers.*

Chapter 7:

The Blessing of True Integrity

*David shepherded them with integrity of heart;
with skillful hands he led them.
Psalm 78:72*

I was never taught *integrity* growing up. I was taught to do good, I was taught to be nice, I was taught to respect adults, and I was taught to say thank you, etc. But like a lot of people, I'm sure, I was taught to do all those things when other people were watching. When we were in public, when we had guests over. You get the idea. Don't get me wrong, my parents were people of integrity. My mother is a saint! She would not take a napkin from the restaurant counter to wrap her gum in without first asking if she could have one. So, understand that it wasn't that I didn't see it, I just didn't understand it.

Growing up, my family, including my aunts uncles, cousins, in-laws and outlaws (and yes we actually had quite a few of those), but my family was very large growing up. It was not uncommon for us to have some of my cousins spending the weekend with us, or us staying with them quite often. We had so many that most of the time, my mother didn't even know they were there until the second or third day. Not because she didn't pay attention but because when I was a kid, we had this amazing thing called imagination that forced us outside of our house and into the world around us. That's why this generation that has the greatest technology cannot even produce a movie script that is original. We have series upon series of remakes, because no one can think. But that's a different book.

One time I remember growing up, when I was around 9 years old, my younger brother, around the age of 5 had our cousin spend the night. I arose one Saturday morning to find them sleeping in the back yard.

No tent.
No sleeping bag.
No blanket.
No pillow.

Wearing the same pants, shirt and shoes they had played in the entire day previously. The legitimately played from daylight until dark, and was so worn out, that they made it back to our yard, and just laid there and slept all night. True story. This was my environment, and it afforded me the opportunities to indulge myself in all things mischievous. We looked for things to discover. We lived for the thrill of adventure. We threw rocks at cop cars, and ran as fast as we could. We ripped shingles off the garage and threw them at each other pretending they were ninja stars. We jumped off the roof onto each other because that was the greatest "top rope" we had and since Hulk Hogan could do it, so could we! We put pennies on the train tracks and hid and watched, fearful that the train might actually derail as we were told by our protective parents (It didn't). And we stole things.

We stole things from the local stores simply because we liked the rush of stealing. We stole things that we had absolutely no need for. We just were boys, looking for something to do. That stage in my life developed in me what I later discovered to be a poverty spirit.

I began to look at things in stores, and if I didn't have them, I would begin to get angry that our family didn't have the money to buy them, and so I would plan a way to steal the item and make it mine. That mentality warped me. It was further enlivened when I was introduced to Southern Pentecostal, "good ole boy" religion that really emphasized what you present on Sunday, and (at least where I was raised), put little emphasis on what you had in your refrigerator, or hidden under your mattress, or who you were sleeping with. This kind of flippant acceptance of integral disregard allowed a generation of Christians to forfeit any momentum that the generation before them had engendered. It was virtually taught that you put on your best dress, your nicest clothes, your perfume, and your best smile, and you learn cliché terms such as "I'm just wonderful, and you?", "I am so blessed", "Glory to God, this day couldn't get any better."

Someone stab me in the brain with a dull spoon! We forced fakeness and called it "faith speaking". Whatever you call it, it became a license to disregard, dismiss or push aside the necessity of integrity. But integrity in the scriptures carries great weight of value, especially in regards to walking in God's intended blessing for your life.

"My worth to God in public is what I am in private." – Oswald Chambers

There must come a point in your life where you receive the revelation that the standards you hold to, are what they are based on your own integrity. You are what you are because you decide to be that. A thief is a thief because a thief has weighed the options and given preference to the desire to steal. But integrity is who you really are when there is no one around, and you can get away with anything you want. What course of action you take, based on the warfare of the mind that you deal with defines if you are a person of integrity or not.

Integrity is simply defined as: "a firm adherence to a code of especially moral values: incorruptibility; an unimpaired condition: soundness; the quality or state of being complete or undivided. *SELAH*

Integrity is NOT *consistency*, because you can be consistently immoral.

Psalm 78:70-72
He chose David his servant and took him from the sheep pens; from tending the sheep he brought him to be the shepherd of his people Jacob, of Israel his inheritance. And

David shepherded them with integrity of heart; with skillful hands he led them.

*"Your **integrity** means doing the right thing when nobody's looking. There are too many people who think that the only thing that's right is to get by, and the <u>only thing that's wrong is to get caught</u>." J.C. Watts*

I believe that you haven't even tested your own integrity until you're in a situation where you have to ask yourself, "What would I do if I knew I never would be found out"? What would you do if you knew no one would see your computer web browsing? What would you do, men of God, if you were out of town on a business trip, and that woman in the lobby of the hotel started flirting with you? What would you do if someone sitting next to you on a bench at the mall got up and walked off and a twenty dollar bill fell out of their pocket right there on the seat next to you? What would you do, teenager, if daddy left his "secret stash" of pills, or marijuana, or maybe he left his twelve pack of PBR in the fridge? What would you do? Because we are all good when people are watching.

When I was a teenager it was said this way, "we all have state trooper Christianity; we all speed until we see the Law, and then we slow down, until he's out of sight; and then we speed back up." When you're sitting on the couch flipping through the stations, and the "edited" version of some soft porn, demoralizing show is on, and no one is there to confront you, what do you do? Is there an enticement on the inside of you that pulls you to indulge in this simply because "no one will know"?

These are questions that need to be answered, and they need to be answered by you!

God loves people of integrity, because Jehovah is a God of integrity. Look at what the Psalmist says of God:

Psalm 1:1-3
Blessed is the man that walketh not in the counsel of the ungodly, nor standeth in the way of sinners, nor sitteth in the seat of the scornful. But his delight is in the law of the LORD; and in his law doth he meditate day and night. And he shall be like a tree planted by the rivers of water, that bringeth forth his

fruit in his season; his leaf also shall not wither; and whatsoever he doeth shall prosper.

The reason we need men and women of integrity is because we need trees. Because trees are good for fruit and shade, but the real reason we need trees is because trees are for climbing. A strong tree gets you higher!

Daniel 1:1-21

In the third year of the reign of Jehoiakim king of Judah, Nebuchadnezzar king of Babylon came to Jerusalem and besieged it. And the Lord gave Jehoiakim king of Judah into his hand, with some of the articles of the house of God, which he carried into the land of Shinar to the house of his god; and he brought the articles into the treasure house of his god.

Then the king instructed Ashpenaz, the master of his eunuchs, to bring some of the children of Israel and some of the king's descendants and some of the nobles, young men in whom *there was* no blemish, but good-looking, gifted in all wisdom, possessing knowledge and quick to understand, who *had* ability to serve in the king's palace, and whom they might teach the language and literature of the Chaldeans. And the king appointed for them a daily provision of the king's delicacies and of the wine which he drank, and three years of training for them, so that at the end of *that time* they might serve before the king.

Now from among those of the sons of Judah were Daniel, Hananiah, Mishael, and Azariah. To them the chief of the eunuchs gave names: he gave Daniel *the name* Belteshazzar; to Hananiah, Shadrach; to Mishael, Meshach; and to Azariah, Abed-Nego. But Daniel purposed in his heart that he would not defile himself with the portion of the king's delicacies, nor with the wine which he drank; therefore he requested of the chief of the eunuchs that he might not defile himself.

Now God had brought Daniel into the favor and goodwill of the chief of the eunuchs. And the chief of the eunuchs said to Daniel, "I fear my lord the king, who has appointed your food and drink. For why should he see your faces looking worse than the young men who *are* your age? Then you would endanger my head before the king." So Daniel said to the steward whom the chief of the eunuchs had set over Daniel, Hananiah,

Mishael, and Azariah, "Please test your servants for ten days, and let them give us vegetables to eat and water to drink. Then let our appearance be examined before you, and the appearance of the young men who eat the portion of the king's delicacies; and as you see fit, *so* deal with your servants."

So he consented with them in this matter, and tested them ten days. And at the end of ten days their features appeared better and fatter in flesh than all the young men who ate the portion of the king's delicacies. Thus the steward took away their portion of delicacies and the wine that they were to drink, and gave them vegetables. As for these four young men, God gave them knowledge and skill in all literature and wisdom; and Daniel had understanding in all visions and dreams.

Now at the end of the days, when the king had said that they should be brought in, the chief of the eunuchs brought them in before Nebuchadnezzar. Then the king interviewed them, and among them all none was found like Daniel, Hananiah, Mishael, and Azariah; therefore they served before the king. And in all matters of wisdom *and* understanding about which the king examined them, he found them ten times better than all the magicians *and* astrologers who *were* in all his realm. Thus Daniel continued until the first year of King Cyrus.

Blessings that are attached to walking in integrity:

1. The blessing of true Integrity is that you are prepared for ANY trial.

Verses 3 & 4 again say, "Then the king instructed Ashpenaz, the master of his eunuchs, to bring some of the children of Israel and some of the king's descendants and some of the nobles, ⁴ young men in whom *there was* no blemish, but good-looking, gifted in all wisdom, possessing knowledge and quick to understand, who *had* ability to serve in the king's palace, and whom they might teach the language and literature of the Chaldeans.

Look at this; the Pagan King was looking for young men who were:
- Noble – "Of Judah's royal family, and other noble families"
- Strong
- Healthy

- Good looking
- Well versed in learning
- Gifted with knowledge
- Gifted with good judgment
- Suited to serve within the royal palace.

This is what the king wanted. And he did not love the Lord. Integrity is not just for church!! It will bless you in the world you live in just as much as it will in the church you attend. Notice that the willingness of these boys to maintain the appearance of godliness actually benefitted them to prosper in a pagan society. They took care of themselves. They did not indulge in compromise.

One of the greatest struggles with ministry is teaching people that geography does not eliminate integrity. As a youth pastor for many years, I hated spring break. Because the definition of "spring break" to a Christian teen in my church was "We don't have to be good for a week, yippy!!!!" And the following Wednesday, every last one of them in the altar crying their eyes out because they either felt guilty, or (most of the time) got caught doing something outrageously stupid. Geography does not change the standards of God for your life.

These boys were living in a foreign culture, with foreign influences, and it would have been very easy for them to acquiesce to the pressures of the culture.

But they didn't.

We have no idea what this is. If this scenario were to happen today in America, 95% of Christian teens and young adults would not even be considered because most all of them just want to skate, eat, watch Netflix and wait on God to open their "door of ministry". If I meet another "Nazirite", who is really just a lazy bum who won't get a haricut, I think I'll throw up! Listen, if you grow their hair out and don't bathe, it's not called a Nazirite vow, it's called laziness. It's called nasty. They call it waiting on God; I call it a welfare mentality.

Because you need to understand that your covenant with God forces you to be what you're supposed to be, and to be ready for it at all times. In the Bible, they teach about taking care of your body, and not being obese. In America, you can be lazy, fat, and die of a heart attack **in the pulpit** while you are preaching, and no one have one single problem with that. But if you get a tattoo you're burning in hell fire damnation.

There is something to be said about being people of integrity.

Having integrity understands that your body is the temple of the Holy Spirit. People of integrity understand that fasting is actually a Biblical command and a part of who we are, and if I chose to not do it, I am in rebellion, and rebellion is sin towards God. *But my flesh loves McDonalds.*

Proverbs 24:30-34
  I walked by the field of a lazy person, the vineyard of one with no common sense. I saw that it was overgrown with nettles. It was covered with weeds, and its walls were broken down. Then, as I looked and thought about it, I learned this lesson: *A little extra sleep, a little more slumber, a little folding of the hands to rest—* then poverty will pounce on you like a bandit; scarcity will attack you like an armed robber.

It's taking care of the things that are important even when you don't understand or agree that they are important. It is understanding that faith is not *hoping* you win something from God, like the lottery. But that faith is conducting yourself according to what he said *in spite of* what the circumstances look like.

Because this is reality; you will not get a job just sitting around waiting on someone to call you. Your car will not fix itself. Stop waiting "by faith" on someone to give you a car, and learn how to fix what you have. When asked why they stayed married so long, the old timers would say, "Because in my day, when you broke something you fixed it, you didn't just throw it out and get a new one."

Proverbs 12:12
  Thieves are jealous of each other's loot, but the godly are well rooted and bear their own fruit.

These boys in this scripture were selected because they were ready for any trial. They had correctly stewarded over their lives when no one wanted them and now the King of Babylon wants them in his courts!! Do you see this? That's a big deal. That's the blessing of walking in true integrity.

2. True integrity is secure in identity

Let's talk about identity.

Verse 7 said, "To them the chief of the eunuchs gave names: he gave Daniel *the name* Belteshazzar; to Hananiah, Shadrach; to Mishael, Meshach; and to Azariah, Abed-Nego.

Daniel means **"God is Judge"**, that's a beautiful identification to be called by. However, the pagan eunuch re-identified him as *Belteshazzar*, which means "Prince of Bel" (The chief god of Babylon). Hananiah's Hebrew name means *"gift of the Lord"*. Again, a beautiful identification of who you are. However, his slave name was *Shadrach*, which means "Commander of Aku (the moon god). Mishael's name means **"Who is what God is"** (not as a question but a statement)! However, his slave name, *Meschach*, means "Who is as Aku (the moon god). Azariah's name means *"whom Jehovah helps"*, but his slave name, *Abednego*, means "slave of Nego, the god of science and literature".

There is a great blessing found in walking in integrity, and that being that you will walk in the confidence of knowing who you are. When old things pass away and all things become new, and that old man is so literally dead that when you talk about the old you, you do it in third person! Jesus help us to see that when we walk in integrity, God identifies us, and it doesn't matter what the world labels us!

"Because one believes in oneself, one doesn't try to convince others. Because one is content with oneself, one doesn't need others' approval. Because one accepts oneself, the whole world accepts him or her." — Lao Tzu

When you are genuine, it eliminates the need to perform for acceptance. I am who I am in private just the same as I am in public. There is no switch I hit to become something, or someone else. I'm confident in who I am because I am hiding nothing from no one. I walk in integrity, and it frees me to be …. me.

3. The heart

The third blessing attached to living a life of integrity has to do with the heart. Look at Verse 8 again, *"But Daniel purposed in his heart that he would not defile himself with the portion of the king's delicacies, nor with the wine which he drank.*

"He that has doctrinal knowledge and speculation only, without affection, never is engaged in the business of religion."
Jonathan Edwards

But there came a time where we were satisfied with fakeness. And we were content with making you think we were right, when really we were just tired of pretending to be something that costs us time and effort that we didn't want to give. So, when we could no longer live **holy in our hearts**, we began to institute a set of rules and guidelines to govern us so that we would, at the least, look holy on the outside.

This is such a sad display of what the American Christian model has reduced itself to become palatable to the surging cry of materialism, compromise, lethargy and sin. Following the rules never made anyone righteous. It simply soothed the pain of the rebellion. It simply frustrated us knowing that however hard we strive, there will eventually be a day when we slip and fall, or mess up, or lose momentum, or lose focus. The issue of the heart was the necessary component to solidify God's intentional pursuit of man. The law could never have done that for us. The apostle Paul even teaches us in Romans 3:20 that, *"by the law is the knowledge of sin"*. That if it were not for the law, I wouldn't even know I was in error.

It is only by our integrity that we show our true righteousness. And the crazy thing about that is that no one gets to see that but God. And what's even crazier is that He's the only one whose opinion matters!

> *"I kick and I scream, I tell you, 'you're mean', and you don't leave. 'Cause when you're not what I want, you're still all that I need, and you won't leave." – Jason Upton*

Remember: Integrity is defined as: "a firm adherence to a code of especially moral values: incorruptibility; an unimpaired condition: soundness; the quality or state of being complete or undivided. True integrity says, "**this is who I am in spite of what I am facing, in spite of where I am going, or in spite of what I am doing.**"

Here's how this test of Daniel and the others was a big deal. Notice that the king promoted them to a high position within a corrupt worldly culture. In today's society it would be like being made vice president of a large corporation. Although they did nothing like the Babylonians, their integrity positioned them for favor. The King then provides a daily diet of steak and wine. Seriously!?

Steak and wine...

Daily...

This alone seems like a great incentive for the promotion in my book. Not only do you get to serve in the court of the king, but now, you no longer have to eat fruit, and berries, and wheat, and flat cakes; you get steak and wine... everyday... Not just when you get your income tax back and you can splurge a little. The favor afforded them luxuries that seemed to be very enticing. And the Devil, along with every single demon that was given your name as an assignment to destroy on the day you were born understand the appeal of the appetite. Satan knows that if he can appeal to your fleshly desires through your senses, he can really get you to focus on the compromise in front of you. Let me prove it to you this way; how many times have you gotten up on thanksgiving and momma had already been up and the turkey was already cooking, and your nose led you to the kitchen? That smell made your body move involuntarily into a room with a crazy woman holding a carving knife, and prompted you to attempt to sneak a piece of that delicious turkey prior to the advent of dinner time.

We are completely captivated by the sight of beautiful things. Satan uses music to entice our mind through our hearing. He uses sexual perversion to entice our sense of touch. And for us to indulge in our sensory lusts is a temporarily amazing feeling. It really is amazing. But it also really is temporary. Think about it this way; when you were young teenagers and when you first met that one that made every sensory factor inside of you absolutely hit the roof with desire….

Do you remember that? Yeah me too! That's called sensory enticement. God gave you your senses, and Satan tries to pervert you through them. The King's meal compared to what the salves were eating is a "no comparison" kind of day. The big raise at the company sounds amazing compared to continuing to be the low man on the totem pole. But at what price does it come to you? Steak, compared to grain, fruits, nuts and berries is a no brainer. Just as CEO , business trips, golf games, company car compared to mopping floors, or changing oil, or emptying trash cans, or flipping burgers also seems like a "no brainer". But at what cost are you prostituting yourself?

Because the first day of my compromise, the first day of eating steak would have been amazing! Medium rare and bring me some A1 steak sauce. Maybe a sweet potato with Brown sugar and melted butter running down the side of it! I would be loving it, especially if the day before my ration was four blueberries and a flat bread cake. But what happens next is that you wake up the next day, go in to have breakfast, and… Steak….. And wine. Later you walk into the courts to have lunch: steak and wine.

This is just like compromise. I have personally counseled numerous young people and said we didn't feel that the person they were interested in were emotionally ready for each other, and that they need to give it at least a month before they even think about dating, and they do it anyway, and three months later thy are a basket case of emotions. Maybe you take that promotion, or job that you know you cannot do well, because your integrity would be compromised, and you take it anyway, because the incentive package looks way better. And then six months later you are begging God to demote you. Literally.

Integrity is a heart issue. And the enemy wants to know, how much are you for sale for?

And one of the greatest tests of integrity is familiarity of location. Think of it this way; when teenagers get out from under parents eye, or their parent's house, they lose their minds. And look, if you're a teenager reading this, don't worry, your parents did the same thing too, they've just learned to hide it better than you can. It's like there is a magic portal that when crossed over the city limit into Panama City Beach (or wherever your teens go), that when they crossed that imaginary line, it stripped you of all Christian value and you forgot that you were even saved.

Daniel is in an unfamiliar land. He could get away with anything he wanted to do, and no one was there to throw conviction on him, call him to the carpet, or even bat an eye concerning his behavior. No one knew, and no one cared. This begs us to ask a deep, self-analyzing question; Why? What is it that is inside of Daniel that is not in us that would cause him to want to live a life of morality in a secret place, when we look for loopholes to get out of having to live holy?

Daniel, to this day, represents one of the greatest stories of integrity in the Bible. That there was something on the inside of him that moved when he was faced with an opportunity to compromise his standards. He remains one of my heroes because his environment didn't change him, he changed his environment.

Imagine yourself there. "Just eat the meat".

It's just meat….

"Drink the wine."

But wine, in this story, represents to us, "any indulgence that is simply un-necessary to you." Wine was given to keep you in a semi-intoxicated state to numb you to your surroundings. This is the message of compromise of your integrity. That the devil wants you to get so caught up on your freedom, that your "freedom" actually entraps you and feeds you into dullness. Not that the wine itself was bad. We use this excuse all day long to justify our indulgences by saying things like, "I'm free from the law: or "I'm in a new covenant, therefore all things are permissible." Which is true, but the verse does not end there. "…not all things are beneficial."

Most of us really only use that scripture to defend the things we do that are truly not beneficial to us. Wine, or whatever it is that you are compromising with, is simply an un-necessary indulgence. It's not inherently evil, therefore tolerable for us, but the devil uses it as a means in which to dull you to reality, and get your guard down for more compromise.

If you've ever seen the movie, "Braveheart", towards the end of the movie when the hero of the story has been captured and imprisoned, he is visited by the princess. She attempts to give him a mixture of drink and says to him that if he drinks it, it will "dull your pain". His reply is something I wish we, as Christians would learn to embrace. He replies to her, "no, it will numb my wits, and I must have all of them."

Can you hear the voice of the devil? He is whispering in your ear, "Come on, this will dull the pain you go through". This will cause it to "not hurt" as much. But what he's really doing, is keeping in the chains of the curse, so you will never walk in blessing.

> *"Jesus. Lips cracked and mouth of cotton. Throat so dry he couldn't swallow, and voice so hoarse he could scarcely speak. He is thirsty. To find the last time moisture touched these lips you need to rewind a dozen hours to the meal in the upper room. Since tasting that cup of wine, Jesus has been beaten, spat upon, bruised, and cut. He has been a cross-carrier and sin-bearer, and no liquid has salved his throat. He is thirsty." – Max Lucado*

Before the nail was pierced into the beautiful skin of our Savior, a drink was offered. The gospel of Mark teaches us that the wine offered was mixed with myrrh. This *myrrh* contains sedative properties that numb the senses. But Jesus refused them. He refused to be stupefied by the drugs, opting instead to feel the full force of his suffering.

Myrrh is an aromatic gum produced from a thorn-bush that grew in Arabia and Ethiopia, and was obtained from a tree in the same manner as frankincense. This thorny tree, called "*balsamodendron myrrha*", is similar to the acacia. It grows from eight to ten feet high, and is thorny. When it oozes from the wounded shrub, myrrh is a pale yellow color at first, but as it hardens, it changes to dark red or even black color.

Myrrh represents bitterness, at least to the taste. In fact, the name itself was given to it on account of its great bitterness. (The Hebrew word is similar to the name given the waters that were bitter when Moses and the people were coming out of Egypt.

"*And when they came to Marah, they could not drink of the waters of Marah, for they were bitter: therefore the name of it was called Marah.* - Exodus 15:23

Hear also what Naomi says to her daughters in law - "*Call me not Naomi, call me Mara: for the Almighty hath dealt very bitterly with me*". (Ruth 1:20)

It was used chiefly in embalming the dead, because it had the property of preserving them from putrefaction (*John 19:39*). It was much used in Egypt and in Judea. It was at an early period an article of commerce, (Genesis 37:25) and was an ingredient of the holy ointment (*Exodus 30:23*). It was also used as an agreeable perfume (*Esther 2:12; Psalms 45:8; Proverbs 7:17*). For many of the ancients, myrrh was considered to be a favorite perfume, said to keep its fragrance for several hundred years when kept in an alabaster pot. Myrrh also had medicinal qualities, **sometimes mingled with wine to form an article of drink**.

The curse associated with a lack of integrity is that you slowly become numb to the things of the Spirit, due to the excess of indulgence in the things of the world.

"Once one has seen God, what is the remedy?"

– Sylvia Plath

Chapter 8:

The Jabez Blessing

"Don't neglect the gifts in you. Power reserved is function suspended. The day you choose to switch on your passion is the day you will see your dunamis power in you. Be inspired!"
— Israelmore Ayivor

One of the tricks of the enemy is to heap loads and loads of guilt on you. Especially in the arena of your devotional life. I may go throughout a week and not read my bible or study but maybe three days out of those seven. I feel horrible guilt and shame.

But that is guilt placed on your by someone other than the Lord. Do not mistake my point; you need to have a sincere devotional life. But take the example of a Navy Seal team engaged in battle. For them, there is time spent in preparation, and then there is time to fight with what you have learned. You never see a warrior sitting in the middle of battle, trying to thumb through his school books to figure something out. *"Well, I didn't get my studying in today"*. No, you war with what you know. And most of us never move from the safety of "knowing" into the war field of the Spiritual heavenlies.

There is a tremendous blessing found in releasing God's word over your life, and then walking in it. Too many of us try to make everything happen reasonably, and in our own ability. And then settle for something that looks just somewhat similar to the word of the Lord, and call it sufficient. All that does is really create a pseudo-faith that causes us to subconsciously have to defend Christ since He "cannot defend himself". When you depend on your own provision, you are ultimately responsible for the outcome. And when you are responsible for the outcome, you allow the lack of your own ability to provide for yourself and your family to create unnecessary stress.

Your last name is not JIREH. That's His name!

Isaiah 54:2-3
"Enlarge the place of your tent, and let them stretch out the curtains of your dwellings; do not spare; Lengthen your cords, And strengthen your stakes. For you shall expand to the right and to the left, and your

descendants will inherit the nations, and make the desolate cities inhabited.

Isaiah 54:10-17

For the mountains shall depart and the hills be removed, but My kindness shall not depart from you, nor shall My covenant of peace be removed," says the LORD, who has mercy on you. "O you afflicted one, tossed with tempest, *and* not comforted, behold, I will lay your stones with colorful gems, and lay your foundations with sapphires. I will make your pinnacles of rubies, your gates of crystal, and all your walls of precious stones. All your children *shall be* taught by the LORD, and great *shall be* the peace of your children. In righteousness you shall be established; you shall be far from oppression, for you shall not fear; and from terror, for it shall not come near you. Indeed they shall surely assemble, *but* not because of Me.

Whoever assembles against you shall fall for your sake. "Behold, I have created the blacksmith who blows the coals in the fire, who brings forth an instrument for his work; and I have created the spoiler to destroy. No weapon formed against you shall prosper, and every tongue *which* rises against you in judgment you shall condemn. This *is* the heritage of the servants of the LORD, and their righteousness *is* from Me," Says the LORD.

All these words are beautiful and great, but you have to do the enlarging and stretching first. That's what's hidden inside of the Prayer of Jabez. It's not just praying for God to do something. It's releasing God's plan over your life as the firing of a gun at a race.

1 Chronicles 4: 9-10 NKJV
Now Jabez was more honorable than his brothers, and his mother called his name Jabez, saying, "Because I bore *him* in pain." And Jabez called on the God of Israel saying, "Oh, that You would bless me **indeed**, and enlarge my territory, that Your hand would be with me, and that You would keep *me* from evil, that I may not cause pain!" So God granted him what he requested.

His name is Jabez. In the Hebrew, his name means *"he makes sorrow"*, showing us that he was conceived, and born in sorrow. And that his name is a continual reminder of his history, and purposed destiny. His name is literally *"sorrow"*. Some of you feel as though your life has no purpose. That you live each day "in sorrow"? That your life has no meaning?

Most of us believe that before we were born, we had a name. A name given to us by God Himself that propels us into purpose and destiny. And while God identified you, even before you were conceived, the devil assigned certain demons to you at your birth, whose only job was to destroy God's identity of you and to place on you the identity of the world. He labels you things such as "pain", "sorrow", "dysfunction", so that even if it is the intent of God that your life should bring joy, it cannot because you are being bombarded by false identity constantly.

Think about it this way, what situation would cause a mother to name her son "sorrow"? Shouldn't childbirth be joyous?

There's a reason why we don't name our children certain names; Jezebel, Judas, Lucifer, just to name a few. Why is that? The answer is simple, because we do not want to attach what those names represent to our children. It's very hard to get joy out of something you've identified from the beginning as bringing you sorrow.

We know virtually nothing of this man, Jabez. We have no idea who his brothers or sisters are, if he even has any. We have no mention of who his father is. We can make assumptions, but we just have this obscure paragraph in the middle of genealogies. And the only thing we do have mention of outside of him is his mother who *"bore him in sorrow"*.

So, it's safe to conclude that we have illegitimacy. And anything conceived and birthed in illegitimacy cannot have the blessing of the father because there is no father to bless it.

Illegitimacy is the greatest weapon the enemy has. The reason being, that along with illegitimacy comes the need to perform in order to be accepted. Many times stepping out of your God intended purpose, in order to be "doing something". Jesus even addressed this using a great word picture in Matthew 7:21-23:

"Not everyone who says to Me, 'Lord, Lord,' shall enter the kingdom of heaven, but he who

does the will of My Father in heaven. Many will say to Me in that day, 'Lord, Lord, have we not prophesied in Your name, cast out demons in Your name, and done many wonders in Your name?' And then I will declare to them, 'I never knew you; depart from Me, **you who practice lawlessness***!'*

This is one of the scariest verses in the Bible. Far more scary than warnings against adultery or fornication, or greed, or lying tongues, or hatred, or murder. This one is far more convicting, and far more subtle. Because when Jesus uses the word *"lawlessness"*, in the Hebrew is translated *"iniquity"*. But in the original Greek, the word is *"anomia";* which means, **"The condition of being without law, or governing."**

This Scripture is **NOT** saying that there will be people trying to live for the Lord, and performing miracles that will not be selected. What it is saying is far more damaging to the eternal soul. Jesus is saying that there will be people who are doing things that, although may not be bad things, they did not have the blessing, or permission, or calling from the Father to do them. They were illegitimate people, doing illegitimate things.

And the father won't bless the bastard child. The Father has no blessing for the one doing things not authorized by the Father. And if the Father does not bless it, it then, has no reward of inheritance. Remember the story of Jacob and Esau? Jacob needed the blessing of Isaac in order to receive the inheritance from him. Just talking Esau into giving it to him was not sufficient. It had to have daddy's seal of authentication on it.

Jabez.

His name means "he makes sorrow". His entire identity was wrapped in sorrow. He has no mention of a father; therefore, he is not authorized, and has no inheritance of blessing.

And he prays a simple, obscure prayer.

"Oh, that You would bless me indeed, and enlarge my territory, that Your hand would be with me, and that You would keep me from evil, that I may not cause pain!"

The word "indeed" in this text is the same Hebrew word, *barak*, which means "blessing". So the prayer should actually read, *"oh that you would bless me, and keep on blessing me, and keep on blessing me."* It's a mindset of asking every day for more and more, and more and more of whatever it is that you have authenticated for me to walk in. You almost have to live in insufficiency in order to really grasp this.

There's a story in the Bible of a woman named Esther. When she finally bends the opinion of the king towards her plea, she is permitted to orchestrate an onslaught against her enemy. Look at this passage found in Esther 9:5-12:

Thus the Jews defeated all their enemies with the stroke of the sword, with slaughter and destruction, and did what they pleased with those who hated them. And in Shushan the citadel the Jews killed and destroyed five hundred men. Also Parshandatha, Dalphon, Aspatha, Poratha, Adalia, Aridatha, Parmashta, Arisai, Aridai, and Vajezatha — the ten sons of Haman the son of Hammedatha, the enemy of the Jews — they killed; but they did not lay a hand on the plunder. On that day the number of those who were killed in Shushan the citadel was brought to the king. And the king said to Queen Esther, "**The Jews have killed and destroyed five hundred men in Shushan the citadel, and the ten sons of Haman.** What have they done in the rest of the king's provinces? **Now what is your petition? It shall be granted to you. Or what is your further request? It shall be done.**"

This seems like a good day with a pleasurable ending. Esther has wrought a great victory for her people. You would think this sweet, peaceful Jewish girl would be satisfied with such a bloodbath that she had just been a part of, but the conversation with the King continues in verses 13-16:

Then Esther said, "If it pleases the king, let it be granted to the Jews who are in Shushan to **do again tomorrow according to today's decree, and let Haman's ten sons be hanged on the gallows.**" So the king commanded this to be done; the decree was issued in Shushan, and they hanged Haman's ten sons. And the Jews who were in Shushan gathered together again on the fourteenth day of the month of Adar and **killed three**

***hundred men at Shushan;** but they did not lay a hand on the plunder.* ¹⁶ *The remainder of the Jews in the king's provinces gathered together and protected their lives, had rest from their enemies, and **killed seventy-five thousand of their enemies**; but they did not lay a hand on the plunder.*

Some would say that she was a bit excessive. She had 75,300 of Haman's relatives killed in two days after killing him and his sons. This audaciousness to expect that you deserve more, and then to be brave enough to ask for it is the very heart behind the blessing of Jabez. It is you actually getting in the Bible and discovering the blessing, and then asking for it, and more.

"Oh, that You would bless me indeed, and **enlarge** my territory."

The word "enlarge" here is a Hebrew word, *rabah* (rä·vä'), and it means: *"to become great, become many, become much, become numerous: to **multiply**."* This prayer is even more profoundly powerful because of the simple truth of who it is praying it. Remember, Jabez? "He makes sorrow". He has no father. He has no inheritance. His prayer is "make great, make much of me, multiply my territory". What territory? He didn't pray, "give me an inheritance". Instead, he began to be specific as to how big he wanted something he didn't even have yet.

THAT WILL PREACH!

We have to stop praying *for it*, but start believing and praying for how big we actually want it. Are you dreaming God's dreams for you?

The prayer of Jabez was so powerful, that the Bible tells of a city, in the tribe of Judah (which means "praise"), located next to the city of Bethlehem (house of bread) that was named **Jabez**.

That *"intended sorrow"* was so radically redirected, and redefined by one prayer, that it finds itself surrounded by "Praise" (Judah), and "Supply" (Bread, Bethlehem)!

Regardless of what you were born into. Learning how to expect according to HIS word over you causes the Heavens to shift and God to pour out a blessing that is just plain unfair to people watching from the outside. God wants you to be so blessed that you are giving away more than most bring home! I believe that about myself, and I believe that about you! God cares about you; He cares about the blessing you walk in. He cares about the name attached to you. Not just what you can do for Him, He actually simply cares about you! God is just as concerned about the *servant* as he is the *service*. He was **"well pleased"** in Jesus at His baptism, and Jesus had done **NOT ONE** miracle, not even revealed Himself as God's son. Yet, the Father was simply please in the person of the son for one reason, that he was happy to be His son, and carry His plan!

Can God trust you enough to enlarge you to the point that you are now identified by being in "praise" (Judah) sitting by "The house of bread "(Supply)?

This is your inheritance!

Chapter 9:

The Blessing of enduring faith

"Pain is temporary. Quitting lasts forever."
Lance Armstrong

As a pastor, I want you to get more out of this book than a good read. One of the most frustrating things that I receive from people is for them to walk up to me after I've poured hours into prayer, study, exegesis, dissecting, wrestling with God, all in order to bring you the Word for the house, and people pat me on the back and say, "good word, pastor." It takes the sheer power of a thousand Clydesdale horses to hold my tongue back from giving them everything I have. Because I NEVER write a sermon, or thought, or book, or anything with the intent of having you approve of it. I ALWAYS write with the intent of having you ALMOST disagree to the point where you are forced to find out for yourself if what I'm saying is Biblical, and true, and in doing so, you push yourself into the depth of growth that Christ intended for you to walk in. I have learned to curb my enthusiasm and respond gently, "It would be better than a good word if you go home and do it"! Always followed by a smile and a half-hearted chuckle as to ease the sting of bite, but nonetheless it is what it is.

That being said, you have absolutely no responsibility to distribute that which you observe or even what you touch. You only have a responsibility to distribute what you possess. But most of us are highly content with receiving a "touch" from the Lord in our meetings, and never walk out and actually do anything with the "touch".

As a man with an Apostolic anointing, I have an assignment to bring awakening to this region. But what I've found is that most people don't like to be awakened. Most don't know their asleep. (No one dreams of actually sleeping). That being said, you may take offense to some of what I have to say in this chapter, but my intension is not to offend you, but rather to show you the standard of the Bible, and leave here spurred to meet that standard. To teach you that there is a great reward and blessing found in staying the course, enduring hardship and staying focused.

> *"Pull yourself together. People among the living still need your help, and I haven't given you permission to quit."*
> *Ann Aguirre*

Ruth 1:1-3

Now it came to pass in the days when the judges ruled, that there was a famine in the land. And a certain man of Bethlehemjudah went to sojourn in the country of Moab, he, and his wife, and his two sons. And the name of the man was Elimelech, and the name of his wife Naomi, and the name of his two sons Mahlon and Chilion, Ephrathites of Bethlehemjudah. And they came into the country of Moab, and continued there. And Elimelech Naomi's husband died; and she was left.

My parents divorced when I was 8. My father moved over 500 miles away for a job. My three younger siblings and I all suffered from that. Although I know his heart was not to quit on us, regardless of that, it still felt like it to children. When we give up on God's plan, and stop enduring, we set a generation after us up for failure. Elimelech did this.

Elimelich is a man with a family. At the beginning of this story we learn a tremendous amount of information in just these first three verses. His name is Elimelech. His name means *"My God is King"*. He represents a culture like the one we live in today, especially in America, whose claim in identity is that they serve the Living God "as their King". He is identified to people as one who's God is King. That seems pretty simple. It gets a little more interesting when we see that they live in the city of Bethlehem. Now, we learned in the last chapter that **Bethlehem** means *"House of bread"*. They live in "the house of bread". And the Bible says that while living in "the House of bread" (Bethlehem), a man who's "God is King" (Elimelich) is actually in a famine!

Or, a people who claim God to be their King, are positioned to receive correctly, but for some reason are not eating.

They are in a house of bread, and they claim that God is King by their name, yet they are malnourished and starving. Understand that it is an insult to the nature and character of God, as a provider, and a good father to be living in a place that you claim has bread, and yet you are starving to death! There should never be a famine in the house of bread. David said, *"I have been young, and now am old; yet have I not seen the righteous forsaken, nor his seed begging bread"* (Psalm 37:25).

Hear these words loudly in your ears today. If you are starving where you are at, then you may need to re-evaluate your claim that He is King, and start to accept the fact that you bow down to the idol of flesh far more than the altar of His presence!

They are positioned in a place that, by identity is a house of bread, and they are not eating in that place. And so what does he do? He moves his entire family to a place called Moab.

> *"I have fought the good fight, I have finished the race, I have kept the faith". 2 Timothy 4:7*

QUIT. THE REAL CURSE WORD

This man quits on attempting to live it out where he is and moves to a place called Moab. Now, Moab was a region on the Eastern border of the Southern half of the Dead Sea. The town of Moab was named after its founder, Moab, who was the son of Lot, Abraham's nephew. Moab's mother was Lot's daughter, who seduced her father after getting him drunk on wine, in order to have a child. Moab was literally born of incest between Lot and his own daughter.

What does that mean? Moab is a symbolic picture of everything that is perverse and out of season in your life. Lot's daughter desired to have children. There's absolutely nothing wrong with that. That desire is not sinful in the least bit; in fact it is the crowning jewel of a mother, to be able to have children! Her sin was to **limit her future to her present surroundings**, and in doing so, decided to **force fruit out of season**.

Her pure desire was stained when impatience led her to pervert the plan of God. And while most of us would say that she is gross, or a whore, or nasty, or desperate; and while most of us would say that we would never do anything like that, we do that, and far worse almost daily.

Understand this, that most of you sitting here today have a desire on the inside of you to birth God's plan for your life. And when you first got saved, you probably started dreaming ridiculous dreams. Like you wanted to open an orphanage, or become a missionary, or maybe just serve your pastor and church wholeheartedly.

Do you remember when loving Jesus alone inspired you to read your Bible? When it wasn't forced, or coerced. Do you remember when you first believed, and wished someone was having church every day, because if you and two old ladies showed up you'd have church? Do you remember when *first love* was exploding, and you dreamed big dreams? Do you remember that time? Those days when the colors were all brighter, and just the breeze blowing in the air caused you to get misty eyed because His glory was so strong.

And then you look around and your present environment is not conducive to the dreams God has put inside of you. And so you then begin to justify why you would compromise, or pervert the plan, by your lack of resources. You start saying things like, "Well, we would do outreaches, but we don't have a regular building", or "We would give more but we've created a debt ceiling and we're banging our heads against it constantly", or maybe, "We would commit to more than Sunday morning, but my job requires so much out of me", "My son has football practice", and the list goes on and on.

What a horribly illegitimate excuse! My environment won't facilitate what God wants me to do. And now, because you look at the present surroundings, and think it can't happen, you then develop some perverted mentality that the church is here to serve you, and make you comfortable, and make you feel good about your compromise. And if you don't like something that's said or done, or the color of the curtains, well then you'll take your 3% that you mislabeled as a tithe, and go somewhere else. But it's a perversion, nonetheless. And when perversion is not dealt with in its infancy stage, Moab, it grows until it consumes and entire region.

> *Write down the revelation and make it plain on tablets so that a herald may run with it.*
> *Habakkuk 2:2*

She births a son, and she, like many of us, could call our perversion God's blessing, but it's really not his plan.

Okay, go back and read that last line again. Just do it. You need to understand that you can call a full church "a blessing", but if you're not healing the sick, it's a perversion of the plan, because the plan was that *"These signs and greater shall you do!"* (John 14:12). You can call a great music program "a blessing", but his plan was to pour anointing oil over your head and if you can't sing on key at all, glory will still fill the room, and people can get healed and saved, and set free!

It was never the plan of God for you to live powerless, and call that "The church". He said, "I will build MY CHURCH, and the gates of hell shall not prevail against it."

Elimelech, whose name means "My God is King" leaves the Bethlehem, "The House of Bread" and goes to a nation founded on lustful perversion, living on dead water (on the Dead Sea). I want you to see this; an entire generation who have self-identified themselves as "children of God", are walking away from the (Church) House where bread is, the place of supply, and being drawn towards a perversion of covenant!

"You were running a good race. Who cut in on you?" Galatians 5:7

For most of us, this should cause something in you to shift. It should force some self-evaluation, and cause us to repent to our pastors. To maybe even have them over for dinner, and talk to them about how you can help their dream. We need old fashioned prayer meetings happening in houses around your community again and YOU need to host them. There is an awakening to start a real evangelism team in your church that doesn't care about promoting a church name, but actually just burn to see souls changed in grocery store parking lots, and mall parking lots, and in cafeterias, and even in churches!

You cannot call God your King, and be attracted to perverse things, simply because you refuse to eat that which has been supplied to you when you're positioned in the house of bread. OR you can just be ANOTHER of the thousands of "Normal" churches in this country! What would it look like if you got so committed to the Bible and to the vision of your pastor that your family actually noticed? That your co-workers noticed? Not that you're the so-called "Christian" Because everyone claims that already! But that you really believed that it was true. Because the Church of America, is closet agnostic at best!

What if you so believed in healing you actually started praying for people who were sick like the Bible says to do? What if so believed in provision, you started testing God by giving all your money away? What if you so believed in the Power of the Spirit, that you prayed until you were baptized in fire, and began to preach with boldness? What if you actually began to eat what you've been given, and started to produce the KINGDOM of God instead of quitting when you weren't *getting fed*?

Stop running. Stop quitting. A bush can never actually grow if the gardener keeps pulling it up to put it somewhere else. If it gets hard, stay the course. Serve your church well, serve your pastor well. Eat the bread that is being served. Walk in blessing.

If you would like more information about Donnie Clark, Addereth Church, and how to partner with us, please visit us at www.addereth.com, or connect with us through Facebook, follow us on Twitter, or maybe even the old way of actually picking up the phone and calling us! We are real people, making a difference in our world, and you can too! We hope to hear from you!

www.ingramcontent.com/pod-product-compliance
Lightning Source LLC
LaVergne TN
LVHW041623070426
835507LV00008B/423